The Chronicles

MW01234991

Darlene Gossett

Please accept my apologies about the formatting. I copied and pasted my blog of 5 years into this document and I left it. It is what it is.

To my friends with OCD, I am very sorry. I totally get it.

I'm sure there is a missed typo somewhere, there always is! I've already posted the stuff in my blog, so it's been edited and re-read for content.

It is my art. I made this! It took a long time.

I hope you enjoy it.

What a love affair.

FOREWORD

I'm not going to give it all away in the foreword! Where would be the mystery in that?

An update caused my document to crash and the computer didn't recover any of the new changes I'd made, I was almost finished with it when this happened. I had to write this book twice.

My friend, the skeptic requested I write a book, for a specific group of people, to let them see what all of this looks like from the other side.

I'm going to keep it real with you, I just couldn't bring myself to go through it again and again. I left it the way it is, even though there were parts I felt repeated or seemed to go around in circles. It is what it is. I'm calling it finished and publishing, because my heart can't take the pain any longer. I can't read through it another time to edit!

I'm going to talk about some things and they are more than likely going to be difficult for each and every one of you.. I'm not here to hurt you, to change your mind about anything, but I will have my say.

This project made me face myself. I had to see it all for what it is, in my face, up close and beyond personal.

I'm not ashamed. I hold my head up high. Whether you love me or hate me is entirely up to you. I'm just here to write about the journey I'm on and I hope my stories help someone else.

I have a servant's heart and a great love of people. I hug people everywhere I go. I never meet a stranger.

I wish I was able to do so much more. My closest girlfriend tells me I'm a buddhist because I always want to remove other people's suffering, without ever considering my own.

I tell it like it is and that's hard for some people.

I'm not perfect, I've got big honking issues and I'm a woman. Can you say over emotional?

That's right. Over emotional.

I wear my heart on my sleeve. I love people hard.

I'm here years later, going over the book, cleaning it up, making it relevant and time appropriate and you should know it's early in the morning and I'm drinking a beer, yes having a beer. It's difficult to look at where I started, to see that person and how sincere she was at the time.

I used to have at least four crates full of writings I'd done. I kept everything I ever wrote from the age of 18. I had hard bound books full of writings, poetry, scribbled pictures, stickers. I wrote about everything.

I only know one poem I've written by heart and I wrote it when I was 24 years old. I recently gave it to the nice young married couple I blessed in Atlanta a while back. It's called "How Do I Love Thee." I'll be saving that one for another book I'm planning to write about my friend's life. You can have it then. ;)

Those crates of mine, my most prized possessions, were dumped systematically into a dumpster, then covered with garbage and dirty baby diapers, because some girl decided I was a piece of trash and it was the only way she could get over on me. My son stood in that dumpster for hours, along with T-Moe or maybe it was the ex, picking pictures up out of the wreckage. She tore the books from their binders, then strewed loose pages for days. She destroyed my writings because I was a homeless crack addict that didn't have any value in the world she lived in, unless I was buying crack from her husband. She did it because I wouldn't let her bully me and take my money.

Huge sigh.

Such is life. You can look at it one of two ways. It's beautiful and worth living and laughing at, or it's tragic and painful and you wish it would end. It's actually both at times, but the pain and tragedy come and go like waves of the ocean, slapping the shore line, forever shifting scenarios like the sand. Screw that chick and everything she stands for. It was all because I wouldn't let her walk on me and because she was such a bitch I stopped buying dope from her old man.

Social Media is destroying the art of story telling, because someone gets to come along and stomp your fire out. Someone else puts their two cents worth in, then another and before you know it there's liable to be a full blow argument going on about the silliest of things.

I'm telling stories, my stories. My truths. Truths change every day.

Truth is nothing more than something you give attention to.

Writing has given me the freedom to just say it. It's my story. You can critique me for it later. I can't write it caring what someone else might think, that's not how this works.

Social Media makes you step back and think about it. Should I really say that? What will so 'n so think if I post that? That'll get me un-followed for sure, if not unfriended.

Where did this nonsense come from? I can't care whether you like me or not in the story telling process. You don't know me in the first place. Those people don't even know me. I am so much more than the things I think, the things I say, the things I believe and I like me. I am learning to really love me. To be good to me first.

For the past few months, every time I look in the mirror I see this beautiful woman looking back at me who is okay with who she is. A woman who is working on the things she knows she can change. A woman that still smiles back at me, no matter what I've said or done to her.

My little sister tells me all the time, "You can't make anyone do anything and you can't fix anyone but yourself."

Words to live by.

Live your life for you and those you love and to do the next right thing. Don't let other people tell you what that's supposed to look like.

I'm not mad at that girl for what she did to me. How sad for her. What kind of stuff had to be going on in her heart for her to know what those crates meant to me and to take advantage of that in such a way?

Do you think, somewhere over the years, she stopped and thought to herself, "Why did I do that? I didn't have to do that to that girl." Who knows? Who even cares? The point is, I'm not mad about it. It's not something I've been dragging around with me like some huge link on the chain of an anchor.

Can you see me? I'm homeless, I live in the woods, dragging those poor crates around, trying to protect the paper that's in them? Yeah, that would have went well. Now I can see it as doing me a favor. Erasing my past. Putting bad energy in the world for herself, because life is a boomerang. Try it if you don't believe me.

I hold no grudges or ill will toward any man, no matter what has happened to me during my life. I'm not mad at anyone. I think it's very important that you know that. Now don't go poking the bear, but I'm a sweetheart until then.

I make no apologies for who I am, for where life has brought me, I took each and every step to get here. Some of them were the hardest ones of all. It didn't kill me. I'm still here.

Since it didn't kill me, I'm good and there's no need to go around poisoning myself with some old stuff that doesn't even matter anymore.

Also, my philosophy in life is, "Don't let anyone ruin you for everyone else."

I've got failed marriages across the board. It's okay, just another series of unfortunate events. LOL.

The point is life is one big journey and I don't know where I came from or where I'm going, but I'm trying to do my best on the walk to get there.

Along the way these great stories come along that can be told.

I hope others find them interesting. I'm going to tell them either way.

Let's talk about some truth. Let's be transparent and vulnerable. Let's tell it all, so it's there for everyone to see. So they can understand, so they can think about their own situations, so they can see what happened to just one person and that person was me.

In 2004 I went absolutely Christianity Crazy. That's the only way to label it. I'd met God. Halleluiah! My life was forever changed!

I was devout. I was joyous. I wanted more. I wanted to celebrate it all the time.

I was delivered from the streets, from homelessness, from prostitution, from drug addiction and I was madly in love with the Lord.

Across the internet, there are some amazing and brilliant people who have been placed into my experience. Most of these people are not religious and have never been. Education is key to what you believe, it takes time, it takes study, it takes extra effort to find the answers. The vast majority of people will not do this, therefore they remain stuck in preconceived notions and programming others have instilled in them.

From One Addiction To Another

When I left the streets, I went from smoking crack to talking about Jesus.

I feel sure most people who go to jail or quit doing drugs find Jesus. I found him in both places.

I was the biggest Jesus Freak you ever met.

I ended up at a ministry in Dahlonega Georgia.

Beans and rice and Jesus Christ. That's the little cliché' they have. You're going to eat beans and rice lunch and dinner every day but Wednesday and Sunday. They give you meat on those days, because you've been to church.

Beans and rice is a form of fasting and believe it or not it's pretty balanced for what you need in your diet. I said I would never ever eat beans and rice again. One night, after work, when everyone else was in the bed, I sat at my mother in law's kitchen counter, eating what she left on the stove for me. It was incredibly funny to me when I realized I was eating beans and rice.

We washed cars for donations, freezing our butts off and starving. They were washing cars, at Christmas the day I decided I was going home.

You will get out of bed at 5 a.m., you will get dressed and make your bed. Breakfast is at 6 sharp, eat and don't talk.

Showers go on all day long, my shower time was at 12 p.m., I was second in line, so mine was actually warm.

Bible study is 7 to 2 with lunch and a short break or two in between.

We ate, drank and slept Jesus.

It's very law based.

You're talking about a house full of women who have been in the streets, getting high, selling their bodies, homeless and you're indoctrinating them.

Several of those girls couldn't even read. How were they supposed to get something out of a bible being shoved in their hands?

If you leave and then go back, you're on a gag order for the first 30 days and couldn't speak to anyone except the overseer and even then in private. I remember a lady who came back like that. She had the most beautiful voice loved to sing. I liked her. I'm a talker, I don't know if I could go 30 days without talking to anyone.

They say it's so you'll go inside.

Their kind of religion is this whole clean you up thing.

They tell you to put on the new man and how if you go back it's like digging up a dead rotting corpse and wearing it around like a suit. Isn't that's charming?

You're a filthy rag, you know, and someone has to do something about that before you end up dying in your mess and go to hell.

You've been out there doing whatever it is you want to do for all this time, it's time to straighten up and fly right, before something bad happens to you.

There were 33 women in that house and I only know one other girl that didn't end up right back in the streets. I even heard the overseer was back out.

I guess Jesus didn't fix them like he did me.

Does that sound somewhat familiar to you?

Religion, the great divider of mankind.

Religion doesn't fix people, it creates a need, it creates doubts and fear.

I became a Jesus Freak. I was NOT a Christian.

There was something in being asked if I was a Christian that made me feel uncomfortable.

I went to church. Boy did I go to church.

I went to church everywhere.

Wait on some preacher at work, go to his church. I went to eleven different churches all the time.

I've been to three different churches all on the same Sunday.

I've crossed state lines to be at church on time, front row brothers and sisters.

I've watched live streams, been to radical meetings where there weren't even ten people in attendance. I've taken the kids to hear a band play, not knowing it was church and let them get stoned before we went, only for them to feel guilty and messed up about it the entire time we were there. That was funny.

I've overslept and jumped straight out of bed, without changing clothes, threw on my shoes and went to church. I've gone to church so hungover I wanted to die, sat my behind on the front row too.

I never missed church!

Me miss church?

No way!

Are you crazy?

This girl doesn't miss church!

I am the church!

So begins my story.

I gave up my addiction to crack and became addicted to Jesus and love and making the world a better place to live.

Today I'm like, two out of three ain't bad.

I have a couple of friends, one is in school, has a young daughter, works full time and doesn't have much free time for me. The other is slightly older and loves her 2 to 4 in the afternoon naps more than life. The third is in Atlanta and I can't visit as often as I would like to.

I have my children and grand children.

I have people I encounter through my job, I have people I used to know, those I'm only acquainted with, ghosts of the past, people who will forever be a part of my life.

I was very lonely and hurt when I started this project. I had counted on the love of those people to be real and it wasn't. I thought they were my friends and would be forever in my life, they weren't.

I don't go to church anymore and haven't for three years. I don't have a support system because I don't have a support system. It's just me and the dog. I had to give the fish to my youngest son and his family, because I'm living in a camper and there's no room for a 40 gallon tank here.

People don't call, they don't drop by, they don't send messages on social media, they are memories.

Not one single thing I believed changed the situations I found myself in. No matter what I believed about god, no matter how devoted I was to all things Jesus, my life was still what it was.

I'll let you in on a little secret. I am still me.

Yeah I know!

It's the most amazing thing!

It's no different than changing your mind about what pair of shoes to wear.

I'm living in total seclusion right now. If you did come by my house you'd have to stand in the yard with me, because the dog is not user friendly and he is not going to allow you to come into the camper.

I'm having to read this stuff again, for editing and content purposes and man oh man is it painful. What the hell was wrong with me?

Seriously!

Who convinced me of all that stuff?

Not one thing came true, none of it, not for me anyways.

Walking away from church and religion costed me everything that wasn't real in my life and none of it has come back around.

Religion gives you a bond with others, that wouldn't otherwise be there, without some other common ground.

I have a girlfriend I can't even visit anymore, because she gushes god all the time and we have nothing in common. She continuously defends her faith to me and I never said a word about any of it. The last time I went by there she said it again and again, "You can't tell me god isn't real." Spoiler alert girlfriend, I never said anything about your god and I can give you hard educated evidence he's not real so please don't challenge me. All that love she showed me when we were alike, all the sweet little gifts and packages and cards and messages ended a long time ago. You can't tell me god isn't real, get a grip, that's exactly what I am doing right here right now, your god is not real and I used to know him.

It's the strangest thing. I thought I would be doing the rest of my life with these people and that didn't happen. I thought some of those friendships were forged so deep they would never go away. I aspired to be like some of those people, they seemed to have it together, own their own businesses, have nice houses, all but their bratty ass kids.

I've actually reached out to a couple of them recently, talk about people not really wanting anything to do with me.

Okay.

I've got old friends who I talk to once in a million years, but think of every day. I've got friends who don't return my phone calls. I've got friends whose voicemails aren't set up. I've got friends. I've got friends I haven't seen in over thirty years and friends I've seen repeatedly during that time.

Today I'm lonely.

Today I wish I felt like I had a friend.

I do have friends, you know how your head gets, that pity party comes along and your mind just keeps saying it, even though it's not true. "I don't have any friends.", what a lie. I have plenty of friends, I'm just sorry I lost so many along the way.

I sit at my house day after day, doing what I do. It's only weighing on me today, because I'm having to share the dreaded stories.

My best friend is a dog.

I have friends, everyone has friends, maybe I'm just grieving today.

I've been through a lot you know.

I'm writing and working on several projects at once, so there's much I want to tell you in several different places. I'll give you the stories, I'll share all of it, the whole ugly scenario and we'll discuss how I came from there to get to here. How I went from being a huge Jesus freak, grace preacher, evangelist to full blown heathen and believing he's nothing more than a myth.

I can never go back, there's nothing there to return to.

Let's Begin

Long before the church traumatized me, it was my mother's mother. I won't call her grandmother, I always called her Aunt.

This Aunt was my mother's mother, having had her sister's husband's baby. She had no choice but to give the baby to them, because you didn't have babies out of wedlock at the time.

This vile ass woman did everything she could to break my spirit, to make me feel less than, to shame me for being beautiful and when she was angry with my mother I'm the one who got the ass whippings.

I didn't have spend the night parties like the ones I went to. I didn't have friends at the house, because she loved to embarrass me.

Here we are all these years later, years after she's dead and gone, the damage done and not once did the family ever discuss the fact she was a legal drug addict. She had three drawers of pills in her chest of drawers, a pharmacy at her fingertips and when she was running low on pills and or had eaten all she had, everyone paid for it.

She was that grandmother who let you know the minute you arrived to visit you were not going to run up her water or her light bill. You were not going to make her late for church and you were not going to stay on her phone all the time

Everything that was her's my grandfather gave her.

She lived with him and his wife (her sister) always.

She made sure to dub me jezebel every chance she got, to make me change clothes repeatedly before going to the bus stop.

She has backed me into a closet with a belt, while I was naked and had been changing clothes, because she was pissed off at my mother.

The good christian lady who talks shit about all the people she goes to church with and bitches about the lady that wore perfume who sat near her. I can still hear her and her friend on the phone, talking smack about everyone in the church, gossiping like a couple of old bitty hens.

She was the first nightmare I faced in life.

I was in the streets when she died, didn't even know it for a few years and to be perfectly honest I was glad I wasn't around. She left what she didn't go through to my uncle and the only thing I got was my grand daddy's 1972 Zenith stereo. My stupid ass ex took it because I wanted a divorce and I never saw it again.

I have been un-medicated for twenty years.

A person's mind can be broken, the same as their will. We are not invincible.

At the time it is who I was, it is what I believed with all my heart.

Today it's almost embarrassing, but it's going to tell you a bigger story and give you a bigger picture into what this all looks like.

I'm still me, I'm just not her anymore.

As The Day Go By

God never shows us the entire picture, it's like an onion, He peels each layer back one at a time and reveals small glimpses to us. Only recently has he pulled off a couple at a time. I have to admit my relationship with God has been in all seriousness and obedience for a very long time. Lately, He's come so close to me, He's begun to joke around with me and show me greater things than I have ever seen.

There are days when I'm out and about and He tells me to take the long way home.

I drive along in the silence, taking deep relaxing breaths of air and looking around.

The sky is so awesome and I admire it every day, only lately He's shown me how He shows off with it. It's a beautiful day, the sun is shining and all of a sudden it's raining without affecting anything but my windshield and I laugh telling Him how great I think that is.

These are the moment of life when I get to just be.

We were created to be loved, for worship, for great parties that are going to take place in eternity and it is in these moments I wholeheartedly understand being in the Father.

He's so close I can feel Him, the warmth of His smile over his precious child. It's amazing and I didn't have this until now.

He uses the wind to kiss me, He brags about the way the trees wave to me from the side of the road and we laugh about the silliest stuff, things that come up on road signs,sayings on the tags of people's cars, things that are rolling around in my mind and sometimes He fills me with laughter at nothing just so He can hear me laugh.

My relationship has become a relaxed familiarity I've never experienced before. I have this inner peace that can't be disturbed by anything and I'm not willing to let anyone steal it from me either.

I wish everyone would take hold of this and run with it, it's so awesome and beyond words sometimes, even though we all know I seldom run out of words.

It's so easy, to have a relationship with Him. I don't have to do anything, there are no fervent on my knees, or laid out in the floor kind of prayers and that's alright. I don't have to try to be anything other than me and I am all He wants. We talk all day long, bits and pieces of conversations, me talking out loud to Him, so I won't talk out loud to myself and some days I can't distinguish the difference. LOL.

He is the author and finisher of my faith, He is my Daddy who loves me, He wants to do great things through me and I'm a willing vessel. There are days when I feel like I'm jumping up and down with my hand in the air screaming "Send me Lord, I'll go!"

Update: Turns out I was mostly just enjoying my own company and delusions.

I can't prove there is a god or that it ever showed up for me.

It's safe to say I crack myself up and have no problem amusing myself at the expense of an all powerful deity, that really isn't there.

To be perfectly honest some of those encounters I was smoking weed and stoned out of my mind, but I still loved me some Jesus.

I really did used to drive around with the radio off, talking to God about absolutely everything.

I really did go to church every time the doors opened.

I really did and still do love all those people

I'm just not like them anymore.

We don't share anything in common and I was probably just a little too much for them to begin with.

I wouldn't miss the livestream if I was off somewhere and I sat my behind on the front row, loud and proud.

I've had fits of uncontrollable laughter in church. I've had spiritual experiences I have no explanation for in church.

I believed with all my heart there was a god that loved me and was looking out for me and would give me the desires of my heart.

I believed with all my heart there was beauty in scripture I could find to help me through tough days.

I wasn't an asshole christian, you know, the ones who go around beating the hell out of everyone with scritpure. I was the one who quietly read my bible all the time.

I was the one who told people how beautiful my life had become. I was the one who still felt like I was on the outside looking in.

I am still the one who tells everyone I love them. I am still the one who hugs others at every given opportunity. I am still the one who want so to join some superhero fight to save the world. I'm focusing on human trafficking.

I am still me. Darlene, loud, proud and outspoken. I'm still waiting for the world to discover me and throw my coming out party. I have a stock pile of paintings I would love to sell. I have Mary Kay I would like to hook people up with. I have stories to tell and am not afraid to stand before stadiums of people.

When you stop going to church people stop talking to you.

When you stop going to church people stop inviting you to parties and dinners and events for their children.

Actually that started for me, long before I stopped going to church. It was little slight after slight for a while. I held it all in, mostly. I didn't want to hurt people the way they were hurting me, but I was plenty pissed off.

I began treating them the way they treated me, like they didn't exist.

I stopped sending love letters through messenger and little "Hi's" on their pages.

They didn't send me anything either.

I stopped commenting on their stuff.

They weren't commenting on mine to begin with.

The magic in the relationship, or whatever my illusion was, left me alone and wanting.

I was shunned by people who claimed they would love me forever. I was attacked by others who simply refuse to think about what it is they really believe and how they came to those conclusions. I was called all sorts of horrible things, made to feel a certain kind of way about the change in my mind and at the end of the day, it was all a waste of time. There are so many other things I could have been doing, learning about.

Last year I learned to be a farmer, got a certificate from Auburn University and everything.

Religion holds no interest for me, I don't care what you believe, I don't care what anyone else believes and I've studied my way out of the entire scenario.

While On The Block

I saw a sad shell of a man yesterday, hobbling down the street, half dead, dirty, didn't even have to see his face to know who it was. I was stopped at a red light not six feet from him, my heart pounding like crazy, wanting to push the car in front of me out of the way, if that man had looked up he would have seen his wife.

It's my own fault, really, because I was somewhere I wouldn't normally be, but it happened just the same.

When I go to Atlanta and I pass the west side I always drive through the trap, I can't help it, its what I do, its where I came from.

I never want to forget where I came from and there are times when I need to see how far God has brought me.

He, my husband, used to scold me all the time about driving through there, but I've never been scared of it. I used to drive through twice a day going to and from work. I've driven through when I had lots of money in my purse. It doesn't affect me now because I've been doing it for so long and if I feel a certain way about it, I just keep going.

There have been many times when I stopped and gave someone I knew a good word, or some money or prayed for someone as I was going by. I used to picked up everybody walking along the side of the street on my way to church and drive them back down the block afterwards.

I lived there for a long time, called those means streets my home and the people in them my family. There are times when I can look back and see how often God protected my life in a place where life has no value, people are bought and sold every day and no one loves you.

I was caught completely by surprise because I hadn't expected him to be on the Boulevard, I expected him to be up in Adamsville, a few blocks away, the Flat Lands. His mother lives up that way and he's always telling me how he doesn't like the Boulevard, how the boys are fighting and killing one another over the girls. He told me he was sitting at the bus stop and some boys came along and killed the boy sitting next to him, yet he's still out there.

That's the insanity of it. The definition of insanity is doing the same thing over and over again expecting different results.

He's been shot five times himself! He's still out there, doing what he does, those instances of almost dying being the furthest thing from his mind, because he's trying to get high. Trying to catch a high that's long past and will never return to him the same way he wants it, but he's still chasing behind it just like the rest of them, listening to that voice that's constantly talking to him.

I know him anywhere, I know him lurking in the trees, I know him bent over looking on the ground for something someone may have dropped, I know him in the dark from blocks away, I know him because I have loved him for the last thirteen years and will continue to love him until the day I die. I can get in my car right this minute, drive the two and half hours there and find him in less than five minutes, I've done it so many times before.

I was so scared sitting at that red light, him so close, not that he would hurt me, but this big gigantic scene would have played out.

I am crazy but I'm far from stupid and I've had enough of those scenes to know I didn't want one that day. He would've tried to get in the car with me, then he would want me to take him somewhere and he'd want to know if I had any money and it would have been this huge ordeal to get him to go on about his business and leave me alone, I didn't even want him to know I was in Georgia!

I had the puppy with me and that would have caused an even bigger scene and then I would have found myself standing on the boulevard trying to get the puppy back or just running him over to get away from him.

He may have come up with the bright idea he could sell the puppy to get some crack and snatched him out of the car to do just that.

When he got shot the last time, he called me and I didn't believe him until I saw the ambulance with him sitting in the back of it. I had just gotten a car, I had money, I wondered if he was trying to get me down there so they could take my car.

Addicts have this wonderful way of burning up all your trust and you begin to second guess and suspect everyone of ulterior motives. There was a time when I would give my mother in law the keys to my car, so it would still be at the house in the morning when I woke up. I used to give her all my money too, because that's just what you have to do in order to lay down and go to sleep with an addict.

When he wasn't home, I barely slept expecting him to come in looking crazy at any moment.

There are people in the street I've known for so long I can tell you who they are from half a mile away, I never have to see their faces, I know their body language, we used to be family, we roamed the streets together, got high together, argued and tried our best to survive. Many of them are still there, even though I've been gone all this time. It's amazing to me they are still there when I look at my own life, how different it is now, how far away I've traveled from that place. I still go to church there sometimes and there they are, tired, beat down, dozing off during service, year after year.

He was limping with a Styrofoam box in his hand, because one of the churches had been down there earlier handing out food. I couldn't see much because there are huge hedges in the lot they were on, which is exactly how I would have missed him. I was going to see an old friend and cut the four or so blocks through from one highway to the other. He had on jeans and a wife beater, I didn't see what kind of shoes, he was dirty and tired and looked miserable, my guess is he was so miserable and not high he didn't even know he was in the world.

He's lost a good twenty five thirty pounds and being so tall it shows. He weighed about two thirty five when I took him home in October, because he'd relapsed twice here, took the car I'm still paying for, stayed gone four days the second time. I saw him walking with a dope boy and a white girl. I didn't feel anything but shocked at seeing him.

Thank God I wasn't in my truck that would have been game over. Oh my goodness! I'm so glad I was in the car.

I didn't even feel any kind of way seeing him tag along behind the girl, because even I know white girls are gold in the trap and if you're really trying to catch some money and get high you should stick with the white girls.

It was about me, not him I filed for divorce after nine years, i just can't do it anymore. I can't fix him, he doesn't want to be well, he's always going to go back and I've got thirteen years experience in knowing that.

I can't go back! I've been trying to drag him out of hell while God is trying to move me forward into something else.

I didn't want to go to him. I didn't feel sad for him, I didn't even feel any of the old feelings I've been nurturing for him deep down inside me, I felt nothing except fear he would see me. It concreted my resolve that he's doing what he wants to do, he's where he wants to be and I'm of no consequence.

Behind the scenes of this God was whispering to me "See? It's alright. I've got him and I've got you too, do what you have to do I won't hold it against you." My peace never left me.

It's over. It was over before it started but God gave his daughter the desire of her heart and it was him, even knowing what would happen and how it would end.

I'm okay with that.

I still lock the doors at night, just in case he shows up, but that's out of years of habit knowing addicts are unpredictable. He won't be coming down here, even though the back of my mind is always saying, you never know. I do know, I saw the state of the man on that street, he won't be down here.

I don't even entertain what he's thinking because I know him and he's using me as an excuse to be worse off than ever before, because it's what he does. He's sitting down there giving everyone advice, telling others what he thinks they should do, how they should go home, how they shouldn't be like him. I've heard it all before, I've witnessed it firsthand and the story never changes.

My humanity still aches for him, I still pray for him every night, I still believe God for his deliverance, but if he had five years clean and a job all that time, he still couldn't ask me to dinner, it's gone that far. I have a lot of responsibility and I've let him have it all for far too long. My life came back around to me and I took it back and it's something so different than any life I've ever had before and there's no place for him in it, because he's left me for the streets so many times I'm numb. It's worse than a man who cheats because at least with a cheater you can compete with the women he cheats on you with. You can't compete with the streets or drugs, it's not possible, but it feels just as bad as being cheated on.

The time came when I couldn't accept him back with unconditional love, when I'd run out of responses because I'd tried every one. The only thing I didn't do was take a two by four to the side of his head and with my luck I would have killed him and I'd be sitting in prison, so it's just as well I decided long ago he wasn't going to learn anything that way.

It doesn't matter anymore, It's so broken there will be no fixing it. He made me a liar vowing the rest of my life to do something no one can do. I've felt so bad about that part of it. I was a good wife, I spent six years waiting for him to get out of prison, writing him letters every single day, I took him back time and time again only for him to leave time and time again.

Now I'm just waiting on my court day so I can be free and change my name.

I'm waiting for the day I can drive there with someone to help me load my stuff out of my mother in law's shed and bring it back home at long last. I'm waiting for the day when God sends that next someone along who is going to be His man.

I've spent a lot of time waiting and waiting and waiting over the last thirteen years, I've developed a lot of patience and when my heart stopped blinding me my mind knew it was time to move on. It's time to move on, it's okay for me to want to do that. My Father in heaven has reassured me He's not holding it against me.

Update: It is 5 years later, I'm waiting for a judge to grant my divorce.

Why didn't God fix him?

I spent 18 years on my knees for this man, had his back, paid the bills, wrote letters to him every day he was locked up. I took care of us all the time.

Why didn't God give me the desires of my heart?

Why didn't he fix my husband?

I gave him one last chance January 2019. He was here two weeks before I was asking myself what was I thinking. To make a long story short, he stole my truck all over again, was getting high in my house, sneaking out in the middle of the night while we were all sleeping, stupid stuff.

I caught him in the truck the morning Randy died and decided I would honor the man who helped me get out of the streets by ending it with the man that couldn't stay out of the streets and that's exactly what I did.

I didn't say a word driving us home, when we got here I told him to get his stuff that he couldn't stay here anymore. OMG! What a scene.

My friend came and got him when she got off work and she drove him home in my truck fully loaded with all the stuff the dope boys now have. A thousand dollar tv, tools filled half the bed. He still had clothes with tags on them.

I was so glad when they left. I instantly felt better.

For the first time in all these years I was finally free.

I don't love him anymore, no matter the professions I made concerning that love. I don't want to be his wife, I don't want to be his friend and I don't want to ever speak to him again.

I changed my number, I even threw out all the letters, an entire garbage bag full, bursting at the seams. There's no trace he was ever here, except the couch and recliner in the living room I didn't ask for he called himself buying me for Christmas in October. He didn't pay for the stuff and now owes nearly $6000 total on a $1000 couch, recliner and love seat. I sold the love seat for $80 just to get it out of my art room. The other two will go when I run across something unique.

He's threatening to come take the motor out of my truck since that's the one thing he's paid for in eighteen years.

I gave it my all.

I gave it to God.

Neither one of us could do anything with it.

It's finally over and boy did I earn it.

What a stupid ass thing to do, to get clean and marry some strung out scrub.

What the hell was I thinking?

Then you have all the Nigerians who are friends with me, who have zero understanding of any of it, because they are so gullible and unread and superstitious, they believe most anything that comes down the pipe. We'll talk about them later.

These fools keep telling me to give him one more chance, to stay with him, blah blah blah.

Sit your ass down somewhere and be quiet!

It shows you how little they really do know about me.

I even have my facebook page set up where you can't say certain words. You can say them but my page will hide the comment and only I can see it by uncovering it.

I'm so serious. LOL!

I discovered it and put it into action.

I don't want you talking about gods on my page. If anyone is going to talk about gods on my page, it's gonna be me.

Sparky has a god of the day.

She goes and searches for a god, then looks at information in the search page about that god. She finds a picture of it, does a write up, tries desperately to make it funny and entertaining. It's not to offend anyone, it's to cause them to think.

Why shouldn't I believe in Anubis? He sounds like a much better god than the god of Israel.

See how that works?

God didn't have anything to do with me falling for that cat, that was all me and neither one of us could do anything with him.

Let sleeping dogs lie, I always say.

My divorce was final in December, I kept the name, because it's mine, I earned it and no one wants to go through all that hassle trying to do a name change right now, with the way the world is going. It means sea warrior and I'm obsessed with mermaids.

I never spoke to him again, I never will, there's nothing more to say and right this minute, believe it or not, he's still in the streets getting high. I'm even past the place of giving a shit whether he lives or dies, because I don't care anymore. I spent eighteen years being raped and pillaged for someone else to go get high. It costed me a car and three years of payments, never getting it back. It costed me over $700 when he overdrew the bank account. I costed me so much more than I can sit here and list. It's over now and my life has never ever been better! I lost my long time job a week after the divorce and they paid me nearly ten thousand dollars severance to go away. I bought myself a brand new life, a camper, a spot near where I lived in the first place, so I could still be in my hood.

At one point in time, I started seeing myself with this big ass man in a wheel chair, he's ungrateful and mean and disabled. Nope, not doing the Diary of a Mad Black Woman thing. He's the monster his mother created, he's her problem now. She's in her mid nineties, can hardly get around and last I heard he busted the picture window out of her living room and the brothers spent $1400 replacing it, a week before the last stimulus came out. We already know he didn't give that money back to the brothers.

I learned of this through an uncle I'm still in contact with.

It's a shame I had to give them all up because of him.

I can't call her to check on her because she'll tell him I called like I was calling him or something. I never want him to have word of me again.

When I got to the place I'm at and started posting pictures someone said something about people finding me. Whose gonna find me? Not him. He can't leave the trap, he never came here on his own in the first place.

I've got a pathway of creek stone that says that would be a huge mistake for anyone to come here. Oh yeah and I want my rock back bitches, it ain't souvenir day.

He's stuck, always had been always will be. He's going to die in those streets, he'll never come looking for me and if he does it'll be the worst mistake he ever made.

I'm chasing my dreams of becoming a farmer. I'm living my life in pure joy with him gone. I have so much more than I have ever had in my entire life. He's not going anywhere, I'm going everywhere.

I'm cleaning houses for a friend of mine, helping her with her dreams and have discovered one of those beautiful houses and the guy who gave me elephant ears is a big shot with the department of agriculture in my state. I absolutely love it! It's manual labor and she's making sure I can cover my bills.

It's important to me because I have dreams too.

Divorce looks damned good on me.

I put him out the day Randy died and never looked back. I began a health journey that May and to date have lost 50 pounds just walking the dog for six months. I stopped trying to lose weight at Christmas and am a perfect size 10 but that's changing every day too. If he saw me on the street he wouldn't know who I am. My hair is white, I was big and fat when he left.

I also know that he imagines seeing me all the time, my curly hair. I've gotten the dumbest of phone calls over the years, saying he saw me, asking me what I was doing down there. Hell, I was somewhere else all along it was his mind playing tricks on him.

I bet he sees me more now than then. LOL.

The Best Played Practical Joke In All Of Humanity

I'm gonna say it right here, before we really get rolling and you begin making judgment calls on me.

If you think I'm picking on christianity, I am and all religion. Man up, face the music.

Religion has killed more people than all wars put together and you think it's something the world should be practicing?

Yeah, okay.

What did you say your name was again?

I'm gonna be keeping an eye on you.

Spoiler alert people, not one single god has shown up.

Millions of gods, not one appearance.

As for picking on the christians, I'm gonna do it. I'm gonna say it. I'm gonna remember every little slight to put it all out in the open.

If you get offended, that's still your choice and I have daily experience with said people, from all over the world, different levels of ignorance.

Keep your god, I don't want him and if you'd stop trying to force him on everyone else the world would be a much better place to live.

Damn.

This is why people don't like you.

You talk all the time, but you don't take the time to study and see if you know what you're talking about.

I learned I didn't know what I was talking about and none of it is true the way it's been presented and I hate to be lied to. I stopped talking about it.

I stopped talking to most people who wanted to talk about it.

Still, daily I was assaulted with the hatred and ignorance of others.

I used to keep screen shots, but who cares, it just doesn't matter to me anymore. I can religious meme your ass to death.

I don't have a point to prove to you any longer.

I don't care if you don't believe me.

I don't care what you believe.

You wouldn't even know these things about me if you'd ever shut up talking about your god.

Shut up!

Stop for one minute!

When was the last time you spent an hour, you know in the secret place, with your father, reading his word?

When was the last time you read it cover to cover?

You love it right?

Why don't you read it?

I've read it.

Man have I read it.

I don't want to read it anymore.

I don't care what it says anymore.

I don't care about your god anymore.

Why can't you get it through your head that I'm done with that nonsense. It didn't serve me one way or the other and now that I look back at it, for what it is, it is the longest most well played practical joke in all of existence.

Damn it I was having some serious mental issues!

So, yes I'm going to give it to the christians, for what it's worth.

I'm going to speak out where many have been tortured and killed.

I'm going to tell it for what it is and I'm not an atheist, I'm a heathen. I especially don't honor the christian god.

Atheists don't murder people the way religious people do, yet some are as bad as the religious, with the nonsense and arguing.

It's from my experience.

It's a generalization of a very large group. I belong to many groups, some of them would surprise you.

The average person is unteachable to begin with, throw religion into the mix and you've got yourself a real closed book kind of person you're dealing with.

You either want to hear my story or you don't.

The choice is always on you.

I'm not purposely trying to slam anybody or hurt their feelings, but I am going to have my say and I'm going to speak from my experience and let's face it, religious people are the absolute worst. It is collective ignorance.

Oh my goodness!

Like I said, if you would stop talking about your god and telling me how much I need him, you wouldn't even know this stuff about me.

I even tell people it's none of their damn business what I believe or don't believe.

It's cause for argument.

It opens you to insult.

It gives them the opportunity to slam you right then and there.

I believe I'll go smoke some weed and walk my dog. That's what I believe.

I discarded that god a long while back and in all honesty my life has never been better. I've never had more money, stuff or stability. Why didn't god ever offer me those things? Why was my life in such turmoil? I believe in god right? I was praying and talking to him day and night. Where was he? Where is he? He never showed up for me, it was always people who did that.

Run Like a Prodigal and the question God asked me this morning

Its gotten so hot lately I'm getting out really early in the morning, to do some things that need to be done, before the heat really starts warming up the asphalt. I'm outside, all geared up, sunglasses, towel, christian internet radio going in my ears, the blower wide open.

What you should know is the whole facility is my home and I like my home to be clean and presentable so there are necessary evils that go along with that.

If you need a mental picture it's half the size of a football field and there is asphalt, lots of it.

Yesterday was father's day and had me feeling a certain kind of way because everyone seemed to have such great dads and had normal relationships, if a relationship of any kind can be normal, and here I was knowing what I know about my own dad and well, that's not what I'm talking about this morning.

Halfway down the aisle this song comes on telling you to "run like the prodigal" and that's when the tears started to freely flow down my cheeks. The same thing happens in the car or truck sometimes, that moment when the dam breaks and God starts talking to me.

I let someone push me over the edge last week and before it was over with my last post was, "Kiss my tattooed ass!" and I left it there and went to bed. When I got up the next morning I took it down and I don't know who saw it but it put me in a place of shame.

I'm listening to this song and the tears are streaming down my face and He said to me, "Darlene how many times have you told someone to kiss your ass?" and I was stunned for a second. Then I laughed, because it was so funny he would ask me that. When I didn't say anything he said, "You've told other people lots of other things worse than that and you were still my girl then."

"You're perfect sweety, you are redeemed. I bought you out of this world when you'd already been in it for a while. It had done things to you, you'd seen things, you had become a person with no boundaries and still I loved you. You're still a little rough around some of the edges, you still have issues and until now you always stand so tall and proud for me. Don't bow down to mistakes Darlene, you are still my child, I still have something so important for you to do. Are you going to let a set back as small as this shut you down? Look how far you've come and there is still a long way to go child, you better pick yourself up by your boot straps and get back on your job, because you still work for me."

How do you argue with God? I'm not saying I haven't but how do you argue with Him when you know He is right? I'm still releasing the dam, there are still tears pouring down my cheeks, but it's alright, it's all the stuff that has no room in me. It's all the sorrow I carry around for everyone else, it's all the things I keep to myself until they have to come out to make room for all of it all over again.

How many people can say God asked me how many people I've told to kiss my ass? I know, I'm laughing too. He's amazing! He just loves me more and more. He keeps picking me back up and showing me the way.

Update: I feel sure most, not all but most, people who go to prison or quit doing drugs find Jesus. I keep seeing it across the board. I know it happened to me. Where else was I supposed to go, nothing else was working?

Can you see these are actually conversations with myself?

I let a whole lot of people say fowl ass stuff to me, tell me the worst of things about myself, make insinuations, assumptions, accusations and just plain out say stupid stuff. Oh hell no! One thing we are not going to do is provoke me. We can talk about anything you want to. We can even talk about your religion in a civil manner, but when you poke the bear. I have no set of rules to go by any longer. I don't care about grace sparing your feelings. I don't care you think I'm going to hell in every religion on the face of the planet.

How many times have you read the bible cover to cover?

How many gods do you not believe in besides your own?

Have you ever really just stopped and listened to yourself?

My god! These people!

There are literally millions of gods. No physical proof or historical evidence one ever showed up, Well, if you believe Ancient Aliens one or two might have shown up, but they were obviously something else.

I find it fascinating the youngest religion on the face of the planet is the one that claims a supreme being, that's more powerful than all the other gods and is over absolutely everything.

Let's me stop right here and say, "BULLSHIT!"

Along the way I met academics and scholars and atheists that were by far crazier than the christians. I began sifting through information and arguments and questions.

By the way, I hate debates. I think they are lame and no point is ever proven by one party of the other, not where religion is concerned.

In the beginning man created god and everything has been a total shit show ever since. Look what it did to me! I'm a prime example of pure brain washing. Indoctrination to the point of mental illness.

I've always looked at myths and books of all kinds, being in love with writing the way I am. I used to read books in such a way, I've accidentally started reading one I had read before and knew it before the end of the first page.

I used to consume books is more like it.

All this truth causes you to lose your imagination, because I haven't written a fiction piece, since then, ever.

Religion wants to dump all this guilt on you if you're not like everyone else, if you say things they don't agree with and when you provide evidence, hard put your hands on it evidence, they will still argue you down. I don't give anyone an explanation anymore, I'm busy learning to farm, chasing another dream that's minus any god to talk to.

Embracing Change

There is an old saying, "You can't teach an old dog new tricks." but that's not true, dogs can learn new tricks at any age and are eager to do so.

People fight against change rather than embrace it, just like the flesh fights against the spirit, even though the spirit is stronger and has more peace. The world is changing almost daily and people just refuse to give up old traditions, they want to argue and disagree on old things and they do. They can't stand for things to be different and they fight against new things.

Change is good where I come from and from where I stand today. My life had to change or I was going to die and all change was good. I live by the philosophy that change can and will be good, because God loves me and has great plans for me.

From the moment white people set foot on American soil there has been theft and murder and slavery and war. We stole America from the Indians, we stole Africa from the black people and now people are all up in the air because the government is stealing their southern heritage and turning it into a symbol of racism. Why are we any different than anyone else who has been mistreated by this country?

The winds of change are blowing and people still won't stick together, they still squabble over the slightest things. They still disagree on scripture and lifestyle and everything under the sun.

The enemy is buried deep in our country and his job is to steal, kill and destroy, divide and conquer and he's doing a really good job of it from what I see. I never like to give him credit but looking at the big picture of America and all the things going on in it, that's what I see.

We are supposed to be united, to stand together, to stand up for each other and still there is the back and forth.

Now everyone seems so surprised they've taken down the confederate flag. All change is not good, but ranting and raving about things that cannot be changed makes people look insane and they don't really even care about the things that can be changed, that are good changes.

The same thing goes on in the church. The church refuses to give up old traditions and the law and move into grace and love.

It's the same all the way around, the difference is embracing the change, either way.

I've got more important things to do with my life than argue, rant and rave, worry myself over things I can't change, when there are so many lives to save, so many people who still need to know Jesus loves them.

Update: Religion does three things effectively, it divides, controls and deludes people. It puts one group against another in the name of some lord. It makes one group better in their eyes than anyone else on the face of the planet and they've lost a great deal of their humanity in defending that hatred they hold so dear.

I wrote most of this stuff five years ago, during my grace period.

What is grace? Grace is when you let people walk on you and talk shit to you and say anything they want and you still show them kindness, you still love them, you still stay in your mode.

Grace is people who make excuses for other people when none of them are attempting to do the next right thing in the first place.

Grace is you can't get upset with these folks because Jesus wouldn't get upset with these folks.

Grace is, "Well you know we can't................."

Apparently grace is this super natural door mat you've become and you might as well just lay down and let everyone walk on you, because that's exactly what is going to happen, because they need stairs for their stairway to heaven.

Grace is the you can't expect anyone to do what they say they are going to do because they are busy and have lives too.

Grace is that fake smile that loves you to death on Sunday morning when they see you, but wouldn't stop by your house if they passed it every day.

Grace is, now be a good little christian and stick your chest out when they pitchfork you and set you on fire. Don't you say anything in your defense. Don't you dare tell them off. Grace is we're in this together and we show up for one another, but don't expect anything out of us, because we are prone not to show up, because grace gives us the freedom to not be held accountable by anyone concerning our actions.

Praise the lord.

Ewwww weeee, I can see some folks starting to sweat now. This isn't toward any one person, or one group, this is toward a lot of people in general in one huge group. If the shoes fits, then stop being an asshole so people won't write books about you.

Grace is exchange your real identity for this one we have in reserve for you, put on the whole armor of God, because let me tell you, you're going to need it with these folks.

Grace is publicly shaming one another in brotherly and sisterly love, of course, on social media when something is said that might sound like standing up for yourself.

Grace is we get to hurt you as often and as much as we want and there's nothing you can do about it, because you have to show us grace.

Grace is letting some ignorant unread person copy and pasting scripture over and over again instead of trying to have a normal conversation, and just loving them.

Grace is someone telling you you're going to hell because of all sorts of assumptions they've made about you, because of something you said.

Grace has never asked a critical question in it's entire existence.

Grace is here let me spoon feed this nonsense to you since you're a baby and aren't thinking for yourself in the first place.

Grace is a weak man's cop out. Oh, well you know, I just showed him some grace, even though he gave me a black eye.

Grace is not what you've been led to believe.

This same stuff is going on right here right now. Like the world is stuck in a loop or something and religion is digressing rather than progessing.

Where is their god?

Why hasn't he shown up to save them?

Why doesn't he fix his creation?

Why does he let little children starve to death?

Why does he let people get trafficked and all sort of unmentionable things, yet he does nothing? He doesn't show up to save the day? I thought that's what gods do.

Aren't gods supposed to be the heroes of the stories?

Why does your god allow little children to be molested?

Why does your god allow women to be raped and beaten to death?

Answer me!

Where is he?

What the hell is his job anyway?

These are things that should spark people into thought and questions.

They blindly accept everything at face value, a book full of myths and metaphors, swearing it's the gospel truth.

They have zero historical evidence their biggest icon even lived.

Their symbol for their religion is a torture device!

SOMEONE PLEASE SHOW ME IN THE BIBLE WHERE IT TALKS ABOUT PROTOCOL!!!!!!!!!!!!!!!!!!

Two weeks ago I visited my friend's church, let's call him Miller, for the sake of argument. I went to my church and after service was over there I joined him at his church. I've been friends with this man for most of the time I've lived in Alabama. He attended my oldest son's wedding and married my youngest son and his wife. He's a person I'm always thrilled in my spirit to see and he's been a huge blessing in my life. I did have a great deal of respect for him until yesterday.

While attending his church the preacher told everyone who needed healing to hold their hands up and instructed his prayer team to go and touch these people. I don't specifically remember hearing him say it but being who I am I just flowed with the spirit. There was a couple sitting behind me who were standing there alone and I didn't think anything about it, I walked over and took both their hands. The man squeezed my hand so hard when he mentioned diabetes. Then there was the big circus show of the all the people who came to the front of the church to tell everyone how they'd been healed.

Yesterday when I mentioned to him to save me a seat that I intended on visiting his church, this is the gist of the conversation we had.
He said someone asked him who I was because they saw me, never mind we were all supposed to be praying, but obviously this person was looking around. He told her who I was and she proceeded to tell him to let me know I was out of line that I am only a

visitor to that church and what I did was inappropriate.

It was like being punched in the stomach,

When he realized it had offended me, he said, "I didn't know you would take it like that and there are certain protocols that have to be followed." He said my being offended was coming from a place of ignorance. He also took the time to explain to me that if I was in the streets, with drug addicts and homeless people and prostitutes and praying for people then that would be fine. (This was insult to injury as far as I'm concerned)

I promptly let him know I come from a place of no protocol and that my preacher is not only my friend and leader he has as much confidence in my anointing as his own. I also let him know that had God thought I was out of order He would have promptly corrected me I said, "Oh we wouldn't want anyone other than our church members coming in here for God to perform miracles through, wouldn't want them touching our members getting something on them, that's what it comes down to." The saddest most devastating part of all was he didn't even try to comfort me or make me feel any better about it, he just finished his call with me. These people claim to be apostolic, to have great anointing on their life.

There are churches that tell you you are welcome, until you don't look like them, you don't dress like them, you don't have the same haircut, you don't have the same fancy bible, until your shoes don't look a certain way and you better not have anything wrong with you, because, well, you just better not.

Grace has opened my eyes to a lot of things and I have zero tolerance for the foolishness of other Christians. It's frustrating that these people are supposed to be my brothers and sisters and they are condemning people, making people feel unwelcome, running people off who desperately need God and are having so little affect for the kingdom.

I sent him a text message later, when I stopped crying, when God calmed me down about it and it said, "That came out sounding like if you were in the street with all those folks you come from then it's perfectly alright if God moves then just not here.

Wow I am more than offended I am devastated and God talks to me too. He would have let me know quick if I was wrong. He does any other time loud and clear. Yeah he really started talking to me for the first time ever six months ago when I put everybody out my house. I am the church I don't play church Miller. I love you don't worry about the seat that's why the church is ineffective no one is really welcome unless they fit into the criteria of the protocol. When your preacher preaches on homosexuality and the supreme court tomorrow I pray your heart recognizes it's not coming from a place of love and that's not grace."

No reply.

My friend of all these years, didn't even feel the need to try to comfort me, build me back up, say anything in my defense whatsoever, I was completely wrong. This is what my preacher deals with everyday, I deal with this! There are so many people playing church and trying to scare the hell out of people that the world is still going to hell.

Grace is a place of unconditional love, the love of Jesus.

For the time being I do not want to continue my friendship with this person and I don't want people like this in my life because there are people who have lots of questions who are on the brink of getting saved and these kind of people spout off a mixed message and all the good is cast into confusion. God has assigned me to be a fisher of men, I had no idea there was a protocol to that command. I haven't seen anything in the bible about protocol and I've read it enough that if I missed even ten times I would have seen something about it by now. I know that God is not the author of confusion and being told this by someone who supposedly loves me who is supposed to be a brother spun me out into confusion. The spirit has never stopped me, not once, and said, "Now Darlene you have to follow protocol to do this." What is protocol? The bible is not a baseball bat, scripture is not to be thrown around at people, twisted up to mean what we want it to, to hurt others, to point out other people's faults, their sin shall we say.

I'll be honest, since I started chasing God the only time I've heard the word sin is out of all the great church people. I've not given it a second thought as to my sin. I talk with God all day long and not once has he said to me, "Darlene we're going to have to deal with all this sin in your life."

What ignorance and don't get me started about the people who are always talking about the devil and what he's doing to them, oh my goodness! Jesus dealt with sin once and for all at the cross, why can't His own people understand that?

There are times when I'm completely overwhelmed at how the world looks better than the church and I'm sure that's God letting me see what others see. No one wants to go to church and come out feeling all beat up, that's not how it is supposed to be. The gospel is good news, Jesus loves you, nothing can separate you from the love of God, you are welcome in the kingdom. No wonder people think they aren't good enough, no wonder they church hop and they can't settle down because they are still seeking that which needs to be found for them.

I have a serious issue with being called a Christian for the simple fact the Christians don't act anything like Christ, they just wear nice suits and carry nice bibles, there is no light shining from them. I want to be like Jesus, the light of the world, I call myself a Jesus Freak or a Renegade of Grace, you will never hear me call myself a Christian. I don't want anyone associating me with that bunch!
I want to look like Jesus, not the people who claim to know Him.

It's not even amazing to me anymore, the mean people who call themselves the church, I'm not surprised by any of it, I'm hurt and angry but I am not a bit surprised and there is nothing amazing about it. They look crazy, they make pimps and drug dealers look like people you'd want to be friends with.

They are posers, they are wolves dressed in sheep's clothing, they are everything other than what they claim to be and all you have to do is stand around and watch them long enough to see that.

I've heard all kinds of horror stories from God's grace people about what they experienced when they were hurting and wounded and broken and trying to find peace in their lives.

Please, whatever you do when talking about me, don't tell anyone I'm a Christian because I am not! I am a Renegade of Grace, I am a Jesus Freak, I am a child of God and if you don't believe me just watch me walk it out in love.

Until next time, love everyone, practice not having an opinion and make your journey too.

God bless.

Update: This same man, showed up on my doorstep not too long ago, talking about Jesus and how his son died and came back talking about heaven and hell. I'm not who I used to be. I've spent a great deal of time learning about scripture, about time lines, genres, writing styles from that time and other historical evidence, or shall we say lack thereof, since I first wrote this.

I never set foot in his church again. He even told my husband he was hanging around with the wrong church crowd. Hell, we weren't even going to church at the time, but don't dis my folks.

This is church folks. You have to be one of them, you have to look like them, talk like them, walk like them, dress like them and believe like them.

He doesn't want to talk about it, he wants me to listen and to believe every word he has to say about all of it. He wants me to hear all the stories about people getting saved and giving their hearts to God and change my mind about the things I believe or don't believe today.

He wants to sell me the dream no one has ever had manifest.

He's even stopped trying to be my friend in the process. I'm wrong, he's right, I better repent or I'm going to hell.

2020 and people still haven't figured out that all talk of hell was metaphorical, the writer had to be sitting in a window or somewhere near the trash dump that was burning outside of Jerusalem at the time.

I'm going to hell. Okay, well I've been told this is across all religions, but hell doesn't exist, so what else you got? It's my pet doctrine, we can talk extensively about it. I know what myth genre is I'm a writer, duh.

I'd love to take a trip to Gehenna, they show outdoor movies there now. I would take lots of selfies and tag each one of them, "Here I am in hell, wish you were here." LOL.

Let's not forget how religion has oppressed women and people of color.

Women are to remain silent. Yeah what the hell ever. What women?

Do yourself a favor and check out the forgeries of Paul, then go and read the letters. Make your own decisions. Do your own research.

How can you use known forgeries as the gospel truth of a made up religion.

The Romans were always hijacking the religions of people they conquered.

Men created all this stuff. Not some all powerful being and if it's the all powerful being they are writing about, he's an asshole and he's going to kill you if you continue to tell yourself he's love and he's your daddy.

I was looking for where it all originated christianity taking over.

The Pagans were happy, had many gods, many festivals, and seemed to be enjoying their lives.

How many of you know there are always the haters?

Well boys and girls, the haters came along and told these people who had many gods they had one god and their god was more powerful than all those others gods. The people were not very smart and superstitious, so what were they supposed to believe?

These guys wrote this book people still don't understand, when only 5% of the world could even read. Eye roll please.

The haters even copy catted things the Pagans did, holidays, festivals, fiest and they started writing rules for these other groups. They started telling everyone they needed their god, that he was the most amazing and powerful of all the gods. Why didn't he just show up and be like, "Yo, I am here. Worship me."

Why all this cat and mouse.

If you be good, I'll come get you.

If you be bad, I'll burn you forever.

That should cause you to question your relationship with your god right then and right there.

Where is he?

Why all the secrecy?

Y'all don't believe in Santa Claus.

Why God?

What concrete proof do you have that he exists?

I thought I had all sorts of evidence, that I knew that I knew.

I was all in it, everything but speaking in tongues. I was preaching and teaching and doing good everywhere I went.

You know, just looking like Jesus everywhere you go.

Asking questions destroys the basis of every religion. Religion is not designed to teach you, it is designed to control you, to cause you fear and anxiety. Religion creates a need then offers to fill it.

Twisted sick men took it and controlled others with it and it's been that way ever since. How ridiculous is it to cut someone's head off over your imaginary friend?

The same thing goes on today.

I've been thankful for the Covid19 experience, because there are a lot of lazy ass good for nothing preachers out there having to fill out job applications and go on job interviews. Their days of being well dressed beggars have come to a screeching halt.

Still the Christian community doesn't question their god.

They have a world of cliches' they use to produce his excuses and cop outs.

After a while they all sound alike and I'm really not interested. I have a few preacher friends left, I respect them and they know my views.

I make fun of it. I throw in little barbs to cause other people to think.

I will never buy into it again.

I've had people spend days trying to talk me into going back, into staying in my marriage, into having a relationship with god. I bet you half of them haven't even read the whole bible, they barely wear shoes or have food to eat.

Then you have the good christians sneaking that rag into other countries, getting people killed over something that doesn't even exist. Oh but they are working for the Lord and it's okay for them to break the laws of other people's countries and get folks killed, because everybody needs to hear about their god before time goes rolling to it's end.

A lot of stuff just doesn't add up, when you start being honest with the book, what the book says and who you think it's saying it to.

You are not in there, you can look and believe you've found yourself, but trust me you didn't. It's a need to believe that arises.

Let's not even go into the backwoods, ignorant, can't even read it preachers, standing on the backs of their congregation, literally, beating demons out of people. They are just repeating things they've heard down the years and trying to bully everyone into giving their money or they won't make heaven. Any fool can do it.

Knowing When The Storm Is Really HIM

I've said it before but I'll say it again, God has a great sense of humor and I'm coming to the conclusion he loves to hear me laugh because we share the silliest stuff with one another and he loves to make me the butt of some of His jokes. They aren't the kind of jokes that hurt, they are exceptionally funny, but there are times when I'm standing there, knowing He's laughing at me and I just have to go through it.

Yesterday was no exception.

I stood in the bathroom putting on my makeup making all the Sunday deals I make with God about the fact that I'm wearing makeup and I don't want to sit in church the entire time crying and ruining it.

There were several times at church I was using an offering envelope like a fan to dry my eyes.

After church as I made my pilgrimage to Prattville for the afternoon. It was lovely all the way from Montgomery, sun shining, beautiful clear skies and the minute I pulled into Prattville there was this huge storm cloud over head, the sun was blotted out and the world seemed to change.

As soon as I got to my friend's house and out of the car, the bottom fell out. I watched it rain and felt the wonderful wind from his garage for the first twenty or so minutes. After that I went and sat on his back porch and watched it out the window. There were great claps of thunder, lightening striking everywhere, the rain continuing and I was amazed. I sat watching and listening and knowing full well it was God. I soaked it in and watched and basked in His company. Great tears swelled up in my eyes and began spilling down my cheeks with the glory of His presence. I told Him how awesome He is and that he was just showing off because He knew we had a pool party planned for 5 o'clock.

I began to laugh because He was joking with me about it. He asked me how I liked it and I told him He was showing off and it was awesome and make it rain some more and He did. I heard His voice in the thunder and began responding to His love, to the sound of His voice, to the beating of my heart. I told Him how amazing the thunder and lightening was and I loved Him too and He made it thunder more and more.

He reassured me not to fear the lightening that it was just part of the show. I laughed, tears flowing down my cheeks and as I watched the storm I sat there with God in awe of Him, seeing His great power and knowing He was doing it all for my benefit and some of it on request. He told me He loved me with the thunder, over and over and again. I would laugh and laugh reminding Him I still had places to get to and people to see.

He reassured me there was plenty of time and I just sat there watching it come down.

I remember hoping someone else was seeing and feeling and knowing the same things.

He dried things up and I went on other errands but the storm followed me everywhere I went and had me running from here to there, because I didn't want to get caught in the rain.

It rained a second time during the course of the afternoon and He thought that was funnier than the first time because it was getting so close to time for us to meet. The preacher posted for everyone not to worry the rain was just cooling things off for the party.

He was absolutely right too.

Once I was at the party He put me in this mode of happiness where I remember looking around at everyone, smiling, with nothing to say, just knowing how much love and happiness He was pouring out on us. Then, when He would let me say something it would come out sounding all hippy and stupid and everyone kind of looked at me strange and I didn't even care.

Anyone whose name I didn't know I introduced myself and stood there making huge mental notes to myself, trying to safely store the names that had been told to me and of course He made it weird for them, because I more than likely did something that made them think I was strange or my silent reflection made them uncomfortable because of the effort I was putting into it.

I would move on to the next group of people and the same thing would happen all over again.

I'm getting used to it, but there are times when I'm standing there in total unbelief that He's laughing when I'm trying so hard.

I floated from place to place, person to person, conversation to conversation and then I was ready to go.

It was a lovely day and words cannot even describe the whole storm experience for me, because there are no words to describe some parts of it.

I love it when I'm sitting there and I know without a doubt it's Him and we are so close to one another and I'm laughing at His silliness. I pray all of God's people have these experiences on a daily basis, because it's so wonderful to be in the presence of my Daddy.

We have so much in our lives we sometimes feel like God is so far away but He isn't, He's right there with us, waiting to interact with us, to pour his spirit into us, to show us the way to the next right thing to do. He really is in love with us and that love is so extravagant. There's nothing He wouldn't do for us to love Him.

The God I serve is living, breathing, near me, talks to me, loves me, makes me laugh and spends the best moment I have to just be with me. He is a fire burning deep in my soul that never goes out and He is my DADDY.

Update: The stuff we tell ourselves.

If he loves us all so much why didn't he stop Covid19?

If he blesses America, why is it in the shape it's in?

Where is God in all this tragedy and pain that goes on in the world?

When will their god heal the nations?

When will their god do something about his creation?

He isn't there at all. He never was. What the hell were you thinking believing this stuff girly?

It was a choice I made. I make choices every day.

If he's there why has nothing worked out for me. Why have years passed and these things I've written about not come to pass?

He loves me right?

He looks out for me right?

He provides for me right?

I chose to believe that.

I never questioned any of.

Hindsight is I can't believe I never questioned any of it.

I learned what preterism was.

I learned what the Israel Only theory is.

I'm not going into all of that, because I really am no longer interested in the scholarly approach to any of it. It's nonsense in my world.

If no god exists, then religion is a waste of time and no one has proven a god exists in the first place.

It's a book club that no one reads or understands the book, but they all want to argue about it.

I never had the overwhelming need to be right. I'm more the "take that" kind of girl.

Hahahaha. That made me laugh out loud, because it's true.

I don't care about arguing about it, debating it, looking anything up to proof. I am done with that. I stopped doing things I hate.

I do lots of other things I find totally interesting, rather than that. I have friends in those places which is the only reason I'm still hanging around.

Since we're being completely honest, I'm usually just hanging around to talk some shit, to get someone off the subject, or to ask a question, to see what kind of response I get.

#1 question all the time, "Which god?" and coming in at a close second right now at #2 is "How many times have you read the bible cover to cover?" That one usually starts an all out war, or gets no response at all.

People side step it, they use words like many and enough, or I've been reading it all my life. Yeah, but how many times have you read the damn thing cover to cover? I'll give you a hint, it's going to be a number that is your answer.

I've read it cover to cover over a hundred times, the new testament over three hundred times, it took thirteen plus years day and night. I never went anywhere without my bible. I've probably read it more than that because I can read it cover to cover in less than thirty days.

They tell you things like you've read it all those times but understanding it is something different and this is usually some genius condemning me to hell.

Yes I have great disdain for it all.

Yes venom drips off my lips when I talk about it.

There's no sense in being a mean ass person just for the sake of being a mean ass person and definitely not in the name of some lord.

People are entirely too brave on the internet because I really am that girl that will punch you in your mouth.

Like I'm that girl that will show up at your front door and punch you in the mouth, so please don't try me. For real.

I've been saving this stuff up for a very long time and Godzilla isn't big enough to carry the ass whipping that's going to come out of me when it finally gets loose.

Please don't.

I fear absolutely nothing.

Prostitution, Drug Addiction and Bondage

You think you know, but you don't. You can't even imagine. I can't even imagine and it was my life!!!!! You walk in around in all your human pride and you say stupid stuff like, "I would never do that,", or "What could they possibly be thinking,", or "They are just weak minded," and various other ridiculous statements about the human condition and what you assume someone else is going through. I'm not holding anything back with this one assume makes an ass of you and me. You have no idea what you are talking about unless you have been there.

I got strung out, my glamorous life as a stripper ended because it was okay for the girls to snort and sell all kinds of dope but crack is totally unacceptable. I was making $1200 to $1800 goofing off, weighed every bit of 108 pounds soaking wet, was being lied to by the mirror every time I looked in it, I lived in room 333 of the Ramada with two dogs, umpteen dozen cats (18 if the time line is right), my son and any other crack head that needed to sleep. I got so drunk at the bar, having my wonderful good time and making money, that I went to the dope man as soon as I got off work, and no matter how much money I made the night before I was flat ass broke by day light. I had to have my medicine, because that was the only reason I was living life, right? When I left they called me scum, white trash, those f'ing crackheads, anything but my name.

After that I went to live in the dug out at a baseball field in a nearby park and no one bothered me until baseball season started because of the black labs I kept locked up with my stuff. Even when baseball season started no one told me I had to leave or called the police on me, because hell, I knew the police, I just left out of shame.

One Tuesday morning, before all of this happened, I laid down to sleep around 10:30 in the morning, you know just to get the energy for my second wind. I didn't wake up until Saturday morning after two in the morning and my dogs were so happy to see me I figure they thought I had died and the people around me were just leaving me there. My son later told me Michelle came in and put a mirror in front of my face to make sure I was still breathing and I hadn't even slept walked or gotten up to go to the bathroom during all of that time.

There are so many stories I can tell you but the gist of it is never ever think you know that you know unless it's about God and He told you, because you don't.

I'm not going to go into my entire testimony because I have a book I wrote for that and you can get a copy on Amazon. It's on Amazon under Darlene Gossett and the title of it is "The Adventure Of Sparky Madness And How She Met Captain Save A Hoe." bottom line is God loved me, He watched out for me, He brought me out and He has been walking with me ever since. I don't care what you are going through, I don't care how low point you think you've reached, He is there, He is waiting, He loves you,

He made you, all you have to do is speak up and talk with HIM. I am not ashamed of who I used to be, of where I've come from and I want other people to look at my life and think they can have the same thing, because they can!!!!! I'm not special, but my Father loves me, He protected me, He watched over me, He allowed me to go through everything I've experienced from then until today so I can give Him all the glory for saving me, for delivering me, for every breath I take and He is good!!!!! RIDE OR DIE!!! WWB!!!!!!!!!!!!!!!!!!!!!!! Get you some, it's your's for the asking!

Update: When did he save me?

It was Randy Bohrer who came along and helped me get out of the streets after God had let me stay there so long.

When did I ever see him?

What did he ever do I wasn't doing for myself in the first place?

What did he protect me from?

I didn't die.

I'm still here.

The dope boys were still selling me dope. Wouldn't a god that loves you protect you from that, if they are in fact protecting you?

Why didn't God stop the tricks from trafficking me?

How could God watch me sell my body like that?

What father watches his daughter have sex?

Why didn't God cause them to be more generous?

Yeah, it makes complete sense, doesn't it?

I've also looked at where that life took me.

I have no connections.

I have a few old friends who are distant.

I have three girlfriends and a bunch of kids.

That's easy money.

Let's keep it real, it is.

Anyway, what a life.

I probably have problems because of some of the roads I traveled, I totally think sex is over rated, that intimacy is much more important.

People love making me feel awkward and on stance to fight them.

That sort of life makes you distrustful of most everyone.

I'm an open book, I am unashamed and other people's stories got me through, it works the same way all the time. Someone has to tell the story.

No one has to like them for it.

Happily Ever After

Funny how the mind works. We think back on things we loved and they are so great in our memory, events, places, food, happiness, but given the opportunity to revisit some of those memories they aren't as good as our mind has built them up to be. They just don't fit into the parameters of wonderful we've slipped them into.

This recently happened to me with a restaurant we used to go to when I was a teenager. We used to go to this place every Friday night and it was awesome. The restaurant closed and we were left with another restaurant of the same sort in it's wake, but we didn't really care for that one. Over the years, having no choice but to eat at the other restaurant because that's all there was, my memory of the former never faded as being the one we liked better. I recently got to eat at that restaurant again, for the first time in over 18 years and it just wasn't as good as I remembered, the food at the other restaurant is better, but somewhere in my memory it is still stored as great.

There's an old saying "You can never go back home." Being who I am I don't buy into the status quo, I don't care what folks say, I don't care if I look dumb doing things I believe in. I have to help people even if they get over on me, it doesn't change the drive and desire in me to be God's hands. Sure, I get stung every now and then, but that sting is so small compared to the joy that fills my heart to bursting when God leads me to do something for Him.

A year ago around this time, I was heartbroken about my marriage I wasn't willing to stay in and clearly remember hearing myself say, "It's not fair, I didn't get my Cinderella story, my happily ever after."

Being a child of God, having eternity to live, what a foolish thing for me to have said, because God's people will get their happily ever after. We have all of eternity to live in! We have all of eternity to party and be with our Father! That totally sounds like happily ever after to me.

I spent a year, a month and ever how many days without my husband. I filed for divorce and paid the attorney in full, up front. I was resolved to end my marriage for no other reason than intolerance of his behavior and fatigue.

How many of you know I was getting in God's way? My expectations exceeded my reality. My desire to be a help mate dissipated and I moved into a realm of

I'm going to take care of myself, I will do this with my life instead.

I know who I am, I know who I belong to and I did just fine operating in that love, that knowing and wasn't even lonely. People came and went, with their foolishness and their motives, but God did not allow anyone to stay more than momentarily, to make more than a shaking my head kind of impact on me and to cause to me to wish for my happily ever after.

When I did think of my husband it was in a shut off kind of way, seeing only the things I couldn't deal with, the stuff he did and not the man I actually loved.

When the opportunity arose for him to be back in my life, my heart and mind went to work, giving me all the reasons I didn't want to do it, a fear tried to creep back in, a voice whispered I was a fool and would end up looking stupid. All these things wrestled in my spirit, my logic, my reasoning, my shut off sense of I'm not doing this anymore.

Over the den of voices, the emotions playing tug of war, the lies being chanted by every force in the world, I clearly heard my Daddy say, "Go get that man." I even spent a couple of more days making sure it was He who had said it and not some silly emotionally charged thought I had.

I was still absolutely terrified when I got out of the truck and saw him for the first time in all that time, my stomach twisted in knots, all those voices in my head telling me to go back home, the walls of my resolve beginning to crumble. He is still dealing with hurt feelings because the first words that jumped out of my mouth were "You look terrible." Never mind they were coming from a broken place, I said them, he heard them, they went into him differently than they had come out of me.
Wow, just wow.

He was not the man I had dropped off a year earlier, although in my mind he was. In my mind he was huge and healthy and well, this just wasn't that man standing in front of me.

Fear was trying to paralyze me and then came the truth.

I saw desolation all around me, the house seemed to be falling down and in disrepair, I even thought he was high for a moment, watching him blow the leaves off the back porch for his mother, before leaving her to her life. Voices were screaming in my head "What are you doing?" "Are you crazy?" "Look at him!" my heart was pounding a thousand miles an hour and I felt like I was about to fall into this great void. He'd done something he can't ever take back in his pain and anger against me and when it was all said and done God said, "You have to forgive him right now, right this second." I cried and loaded boxes onto my truck, I walked back and forth time after time wallowing in the pain of it all. I'm not even going to tell you what it was because I did forgive him and I've resolved myself never to mention it again, just like God never reminds me of who I used to be.

In the recesses of my mind, buried deep in my frustration and anger and fatigue were memories of him, sweet precious memories I didn't let myself have, like how he washes my truck and car, spends hours at a time getting them clean knowing I am going to let the dogs smudge the windows right back up. I forgot how he washes my dishes, cleans my house, says the sweetest things to me, makes me laugh and knows how to have fun. I forgot how wonderful it is to be at home in my own skin because of him. Many many things buried behind the voices and memories and dark shadows that have stood guard over that part of me. I don't mind the TV being entirely too loud, little messes here and there where he's been posted up. It is my great pleasure to cook for him, to see him in the living room completely immersed in a video game, to have laughing little spats.

I've had people along the way to love me and encourage me, to keep me moving forward dropping chains all along the way. Those same people are there for him, to do the same, to help him on his journey. I can't be of any help carrying around my own expectations, my how things should be thoughts, my wishing things were different. I can only see the next good thing to do for him, to be for him, to give to him and the rest of it is between him and his Daddy.

In order to get my happily ever after with him I have to live the entire Cinderella story and to tell the truth it's a great story and all of it isn't bad. To get my happily ever after with God, I just have to be.

How cool is that?

Update: What was I thinking?

I know I wasn't on drugs! I've been clean going on 16 years!

Happily ever after started when the delusions stopped.

Happily ever after started when my truck made that last trip to Georgia again.

Happily ever after is nothing more than a concept, something we tell ourselves because all the fairy tales end that way.

For christians their happily ever after is heaven.

How do you know?

Because the bible says so.

How do you know it's telling you the truth?

It's the word of God.

You realize men wrote it right? Men that didn't even know they were supposed to wash their asses everyday. Yeah everybody let's live our lives according to what the stinky guys wrote.

Why didn't God write his own book?

Gee. I wonder.

The Long Journey Back Up And Never Taking Anything For Granted

God put this on my heart this morning, reminding me of where I came from, how I'm nowhere near where I'm going and what's right in front of me. What a journey it's been! I started in the streets, with nothing. By the time I came out of the streets, all the dogs had died or gone elsewhere, the cats were scattered from here to kingdom come and all I had of all the stuff was a leather jacket I found laying next to a dumpster, a duffle bag of clothes and a lot of bad memories. I was carrying a brand new bible, which I still have all these years later. It's covered in duct tape and a beautiful cover because I never had the strength to give it up long enough to have it recovered and it will stay that way until I'm long gone.

I'm reminded of where I came from this morning as a friend came to me telling me about a woman who is coming out of the street this weekend. She's going to have her own place, she needs stuff for her place and she needs lots of support, from many places if she is to survive. Most of all she will need the help of Jesus and people He places in her life.

I don't know her, but I used to be her.

When I think back, I find I am still that person, still that grateful and humbled by His love. I'm not the person I used to be but I am still that woman who has been rescued every day since then from a life that can only be described as pure hell. My worst day since then is still my better than my best day out there.

I'm thinking of her, what it feels like, knowing that place and how it looks and feels and the opportunity that will grow from it. I remember that sigh of relief that escapes and eases it away. I remember the wonders of that time, the new experiences, the eye opening things that happened and the changing of the guard as my heart became set on something so much higher.

He's been so good to me! I could fill the world with all of it, if I could remember all of it, the things He's done for me since then.

Every time it rains, even after all these years I thank God I'm not in the street. When it's super cold outside, late at night, when I'm laying in my bed, I thank God I'm not still in the street.

It's a long journey back, but one I was so grateful and thankful to make. He walked with me every step of the way, He showed me His love every moment of every day. He stayed with me every breath and I am still in His presence and what a wonderful place to be!

I look at that little green truck sitting outside and thank Him for it, as I have done every day since April 2009. That truck is the nicest most reliable thing I've ever owned and by some other folk's standards that's pretty pathetic, but to me it's huge. It's a blessing! It's the best thing I've got and I have enjoyed having it so much.

I think about her, what its going to feel like when every one is gone and she has that moment where she stops and looks around and God whispers to her, "I did this for you." and her heart soars with the great joy that moment will bring. I think about the pride she will have in taking ownership of her life, how important her shower curtain will be to her, the towels and washrags someone gave her, the frying pan she will use to cook in her kitchen, small things we all take for granted until we need them.

I'm so happy for her, whatever her name is, whomever she may be, because God put someone as wonderful as my friend and many more in her path to make sure she begins the long journey back up and I pray, neither one of us ever take anything for granted.

Update: It's the same thing without a god. Life is short and precious, we don't know what comes next, there's no proof next exists. Being grateful and thankful are still the only way to live.

Life is a boomerang, write that down.

Being Sensitive To Others

Life is happening to everyone, we are all on a journey and certain parts of it are so painful. I'm the eternal optimist, know who I belong to, know He has great plans for me and I'm beginning to see some of these plans come to fruition, at long last. In the process I'm learning about loyalty, about being sensitive to others, about picking and choosing the best things to be involved in and I'm learning how vulnerable my own heart is to the actions of others.

Everyone wants to be supported, cheered on, valued and to have people on their team.

Lately, I've noticed a great deal of the exact opposite. I've seen those who claim to be sensitive to others, being self absorbed, only interested in what they are doing and want to do. They want everyone to support their causes and be involved in their stuff, but they pay no mind to everyone else.

God is bringing me to a place where He is showing me how He supports me and it's never through the people I am expecting it to be, it is always others, people outside my closest circles, people I never dreamed of and people I hardly know.

My heart is more than a little broken about this, but broken is good where God is concerned.

Even still it makes me not want to share with others, not mention things I would like to do, to withdraw to the depths of my own life, my own reality.

I'm not easily offended, or overly sensitive about things, it's just not my way, but when the hurt creeps in it's there and it's so difficult to get rid of.

I refuse to believe I give people too much credit, but more than a million times this has been said to me.

There are those who whole heartedly support one another, the whole ride or die thing. They hang out together, they go to one another's functions, they regularly pursue their relationships with one another.

All the while there are people on the outside looking in, some of them longing for those relationships, others feeling shut out, left out, excluded and forgotten. This should not be so, but such is life.

In the end the only person who does not forget us, who does not make us feel excluded, overlooked, left out, or unloved is God. He is there for every moment, the good ones and the bad ones. He is there pouring out His love on us, knowing our hurt, our isolation and longings. He is the one who always says, "You are okay.", instead of asking. He is the one who always says, "You are lacking nothing." instead of do you need anything. He's the one who is there in the darkest of moments constantly reminding us of His love, the plans He has for us.

For this I am so grateful because for this moment in time I am hurt by people. Update: Is he really?
How sensitive have believers been to those who chose not to over the last two thousand years?

This is why I made it a point to give you some insight to me, the condition of my heart today.

I am not bitter or angry.

My feelings are no longer hurt.

I asked three of those people to show up for me. They did not. I was completely   for a long while.

Six months later my best girl realizes no one has tried to fix that hurt. I've heard from five people out of ?????????

Everybody loved me to death on Sunday. I was everybody's golden girl for all those years. I've driven in from out of state, half a dozen times to be at church, on the front row, loud and happy to be there.

I was that girl. I wanted it to be a like a rave. I wasn't ashamed of my excitement about God. I had the best time out of everyone. I yelled and sang and danced and cried my eyes out.

Damn.

I was one of "them", you know "them". Oh my goodness. You have no idea how hard this is for me, to be totally transparent and lay it all out there for you. Isn't it terrible? It's us and them. I don't want to be one of them   No one ever stops talking about their god.

So anyway, I just stopped going. I just sat back. I waited to see who would pursue me. I know who is true. I know who really loves me. I still have those rare few.

I stayed away from everyone because of the old saying hurt people hurt people.

I was having to deal with the knucklehead I stuck myself with again.

I focused on my own happiness, my hobbies, changing the way I think.

There may have been a dozen messages in a year and eight months. Maybe.

I stayed away from them, because I am no longer like them.

I stayed away from them, because I've heard and spoken absolutely enough about their god.

I stayed away.

No one showed up at my house either.

My girl.

She showed up.

She is super.

I felt completely rejected and unloved. I felt like I was drowning in a whole bunch of bad choices I made and no they did not show up for me! No we were not in this thing together!

I can hear the grace camp interpreters now.

Well you know Darlene.

It's important to me for you to know these things. So many people simply hate me for a filthy word they chose. It's okay and you don't have to hate me.

Calm down, it's not that serious.

I miss the two who count. I miss the two who sincerely love me. I miss them terribly and the connection is still there. The universe works it out where we are usually on the same page, whether we've been talking to one another and or seeing one another. We share something I can't explain and it is NOT a god.

The rest, well god bless them and I wish them well. They weren't my people. The ones who are are still right in front of me. I can only deal with what is right in front of me, reality sort of works that way.

My life is full.

Family is all that matters.

I've stepped back and looked at the situation for a very long time.

I was devastated to begin learning things and then want nothing to do with it.

I've spent 13+ years in the bible night and day.

I don't want to read it anymore.

It's not even that good. A good book can be figured out. A good book has nice surprises and twists and turns to weave the story together. A good book would contain good news. They call it "the good book," "God's word", a bunch of men wrote it and they didn't do a very good job. A good book, good news, here's what we're talking about plain and simple.

The first rule of writing for an audience, especially a wide spread audience, (who can't read,) is to pretend who ever you are writing to five years old and you want them to understand what you are saying.

Randy once wrote me a dissertation about the tribe of Israel committing genocide. It was so complicated I had to sit with a dictionary in my lap to look up words, so I would know what he was talking about.

Which reminds me, I still have that and would love to turn it over to some real scholars I've encountered along the way. See what they have to say about it. The man was brilliant. He had a massive stroke and taught himself to write again using an overhead projector. He said he was an arrogant academic and wanted to make up for that.

He forgot to pretend I was dumb so I would know what he actually meant with the things he was saying.

I loved my preacher, I called him friend. I still call him friend and wish him all the best.

I'm not trying to change anyone's mind or convince anyone of anything.

Find your own answers.

Ask your own questions.

Believe what you want.

I don't care.

If you mention it to me, we're gonna talk about it. I never bring it up unless someone else does.

Today I feel like it's a perpetuated lie, everyone just keeps going along with it, no one is reading it completely. It's like cheat codes in a video game. You don't have to play the whole book in order to participate.

There wasn't a voice for me where I was and that's okay now too.

I can count my friends on one hand. Everyone else is just passing by. No one else passed by this way again.

My friends.

Anyway.

In the meantime, I'm sitting on 300 paintings. Maybe? I had 256 the last event I did and I've been painting as well.

Planning to start listing them on Amazon since my book is finally there. Might renew my fan base or something. Hell, I don't know, I'm always hopeful for a miracle, that's always been my problem.

If it don't make money it don't make sense.

I'm still me, but I don't believe any of it any longer, not even the tiniest sliver of it.

I think it's all myth, a terribly patched together fairy tale.

No god has ever shown up and revealed itself and it seems to me the god of that book is pretty arrogant and seems to be shady about being seen. Arrogance and shyness do NOT go hand in hand. Arrogance would cause a god to appear.

No, he just gets pissed off and kills everybody. Still no sighting.

Oh but he's the god of love.

Circular reasoning is what faith is. No evidence whatsoever.

Have him tell you my favorite color.   He ought to know, we used to be close.

Biting Off More Than You Can Chew

I was so excited to see those huge, fantastic, almost wouldn't fit in the car canvases! Man! All the thoughts that went through my mind, dollar bills y'all! Now they are leaned against the wall in the spare bedroom, so big, they won't fit an easel, "What am I gonna paint?" , "Oh my gosh look how much space that is to cover!", "Good Lord!"

All the while my spirit is jumping around inside of me clapping her hands and excited for the challenge.

Then you have the part where I'm like, "Okay, this has to be something absolutely breathtaking!"

My spirit yells "I know!"

Back and forth we go and I'm still looking at pictures, trying to get ideas, a tree came to mind colorful background, dark tree, a light house in a sea storm and I have an amazing picture to use as an example. The biggest mermaid seascape of my career?

Then there are the butterflies, because it's all about the butterflies and they've come back around as a point of interest. In case you don't know butterflies are very difficult, because they are perfectly proportioned.

What to paint, what to paint.

I   n the meantime I'm trying to relax, to try simplicity, it's not that serious, just put the brush in the paint and see what happens!

Wood burning projects on the back burner because to paint is to breathe.

I'm not going to say I bit off more than I could chew because those two canvases have been a dream of mine for a long time and please forgive me but I have no desire to paint an angel on either one of them.

Just soaking in the goodness of God and sticking to small beginnings until those two are the last two available.

Then the fun begins!

RIDE OR DIE!!!

WWB!!!

Update: I still paint.

I don't start out listening to Jesus Culture, My Soul Longs for you anymore. I don't listen to christian music at all.

I'm a bass head, so I listen to a lot of Tech N9ne and his crew, old school stuff.

I'm branding myself with Butterfly Diva, so I'm doing two piece butterfly paintings.

There are backgrounds waiting to be painted, but I'm writing as well.

All these dreams, hopes, beliefs, prayers. None of this stuff ever came true. It never worked out for me. I haven't sold makeup to anyone but myself in a year. I haven't sold a painting in just as long.

The church I used to go to closed.

I'm very sad for him. We all have dreams. He worked really hard to get to his dream. I painted a painting for Easter the last Easter I was there. It's a huge 36 x 48 Jesus. It was for the building and since it's sitting in storage that means no one liked it enough to take it home with them, so I've asked for the painting back. It's my art. It means something to me.

You can judge me or whatever. I didn't feel like it was a bit rude. I did the painting for him, it will always be the painting I did for him, but if he doesn't want the painting I am not offended by taking it back. It was the thought that counted in the first place. I paint amazing Jesus paintings by the way. Go figure.

I don't ever want to hurt him, which is why I stayed away. Also, I get the choice of whether or not to care about anyone else and while we're talking about it and I'm getting it all out, I have to speak on something that happened surrounding that.

I got bumped twice and to preach twice in nearly ten years.

I was given a voice somewhere else which totally thrilled me and I wasn't shy about asking to do it.

I did a painting the previous Easter. It was supposed to be the painting I am now talking about, but I goofed it and shook my confidence in myself and did something else. I sold that painting for $60 in the fall because the girl loved the colors.

It's really good, he has a big Jewish nose and everything.

So, it's Easter, I set the painting up front.

He doesn't know the painting is for him until after service because it's Easter. I take it over to the building. I used to know the code. I don't anymore.

Fast forward a couple of Sunday's later. A lady had a print framed of Jesus reaching down into a pool of water. A huge production was made about this picture.

It was like sitting at a red light getting t-boned by a diesel truck. It came out of nowhere and hurt me so bad I got the hell on as soon as service was over and I cried all the way to the house. I never went back after that service.

I don't really know these people.

I don't have their phone numbers.

I've been to a few of their houses.

A few of the have been to mine.

Figure if one of them talks shit about someone else to me, they're talking shit about me to everyone else behind my back.

If you haven't spoken to me in six months, were we really friends in the first place?

I had to re-evaluate what friends are.

I have three close girlfriends, a handful of others elsewhere and my family.

I don't want fake people in my life. I've lived through enough of that for three lifetimes.

I want to be left in peace.

I want to be treated with kindness.

I want people to shut the hell up and or listen to themselves once in a while.

This is an eye opener for me. I am still me, I am not that person anymore, but here she is, in your face. A true believer at the time. Let's keep going, see where this takes us.

Stuck In The Loop

The last couple of days have been good ones even though stupid stuff is going on in my life. Living with an addict your life plays out on this loop that's stuck. You go along, thinking everything is going to be alright then they do the deed. No explanation, no way to understand it, no figuring it out and total devastation comes along. Things of value are gone, trust is gone, hope is dashed for a few moments and then begins the process of rebuilding. There's the quiet time, where they are going through it, stuck in their mind, processing all the information as to what they've done. At some point in time, they try turning the blame on you and making you feel guilty about some part you played in it but it's not about you and still you have that part of it. Then , as the shame wears off, they start making plans again, trying to figure out how to fix it, everything is supposed to be alright and you better not act any different. You start putting the building back together, brick by brick, doing what is necessary to fix the current situation, starting over for the millionth time.

I've been stuck in a loop for fifteen years. Yes, for fifteen long, frustrating ,he can never get it right years.

He's not honest about it. He won't tell on it. If you give him some money you have just launched him into the abyss.

Things walk away, vehicles get tore up, he comes in with his tail between his legs, looking like a six year old who has broken his mother's favorite vase, takes a bath and goes to bed. No "I'm sorry,", no explanation whatsoever, but you know all hell has broken loose once again and it costed you something along the way.

I could be wrong, but I don't think I've ever even heard an, "I'm sorry baby."

It's not for the faint of heart.

Over and over again I have to practice trusting, even though I'm still jumping out of bed to make sure he's still here, to know where my pocket book and all the keys are, to reassure myself of something. It's insanity really, doing the same thing over and over again expecting different results.

In the end I'm always the one left standing in the middle of the wreckage, feeling taken advantage of, lied to, beat down, bills to pay, at the beginning of a long journey I've made more than a hundred times. I'm the one who begins to build again, to pick up the pieces, to start gluing it all back together.

It sucks.

It's been going on so long, I don't even tell people when it happens anymore. Why should they care? He's my problem and somehow his problems have become my problems. They couldn't possibly understand the pain of those moments, unless they've been there before and no one likes a cry baby.

You can't say certain things, you can't have certain opinions, you can't put safety measures into place because he's not honest about it and he's not going to share the information with anyone else, because God forbid they might be of some help when the time comes.

I'm not participating any longer.

I'm not replacing things.

I'm not paying anyone money.

I'm not doing it!

I've set the boundaries and he has to find something to go after.

I refuse to continue to live this way.

It's not living, it's constantly watching your life implode, everything you worked for to get to today gone in the blink of an eye.

In the end I feel like he doesn't care, because he never has to take any responsibility for it. He doesn't have a job to start trying to play catch up, the dang job is what put him back in the streets to start with. His male pride won't let him admit he needs to do something, he can't handle money, that it's all bigger than him and he needs to do something about it.

We never get ahead, I start over at this starting point marked devastation.

You have to find a way to live through it. to be who you are called to be, to keep the course of your own journey.

It makes them very hard to love.

Some of us are living in expectancy of an apology we are never going to get.

I've been there so that makes it's an even bigger mystery to me.

What makes me able to stop and not care that he doesn't have?

There are never anymore answers than there are questions.

Married To A Crackhead

After the initial anger and pain wore off I made a decision and it was by far the best decision I've ever made in my life.

I sat down and put some worship music on and began to talk to my Father. I started out crying and hurt and ended up laughing and loved. I merely soaked in His presence. He loves me. It doesn't matter to Him what's going on, all that is important is our love affair with one another.

I've painted and listened to music and told Him all my problems and He's loved me back with such fierceness I was healed of everything. I didn't matter what he was doing. It didn't matter where he was. It didn't matter what he's going to do next, nothing else mattered but God, the creator of the universe loves me and was spending time with me in my moment of darkness,

A great peace came over me and I didn't even care anymore.

I keep seeing all of it as new testimony, new territory.

We are hard pressed on every side, but not crushed, perplexed, but not in despair, persecuted but not abandoned, struck down but not destroyed.

Halleluiah!

I don't know if he'll ever figure it out, but as for me, I've got stuff to do, I'm trying to usher in the kingdom for him and everyone else. I've got territory to take and my ministry is just now getting off the ground. I will not be discouraged.

I believe His promises.

I'm stepping out of the loop, I'm not participating or living there anymore. The boundary lines have been drawn and I'm sticking to them. I have the right to peace.

I have the right to freedom. I have been set free, it no longer holds bondage for me and I'm not going to voluntarily chain myself to it.

Take my advice, the next time you are going through pure hell, sit down, put some music on, begin to thank God for all He's done for you, dump all your garbage on Him and take your peace.

I'm pretty sure it makes you glow.

Update: I finally got off the hamster wheel.

Again I ask why didn't God fix my husband?

I asked enough.

I prayed enough.

I read my bible cover to cover over a hundred times, probably more.

I love people.

I believed.

I had blind faith.

Why?

They don't teach you to ask questions and when you ask hard ones they don't have answers, they just parrot everyone that came before them, the same nonsense over and over again until everyone is saying it.

The One Who Set The Standard

God is doing such amazing things in my life, there are nights when I can hardly sleep. There are times I wake up talking to God, when I was deeply submerged in a dream. There are times when so many exciting things are going on I'm about to absolutely explode with excitement and wonder.

We're all on a journey.

Everything that happens to us is part of our story, the testimony we get to give to others. The story of how we were going through hell and God came and rescued us.

The beautiful thing about testimony is you tell your story and others hear it and this small voice inside them that says "Damn, they've been through it," then it begins telling them maybe they can make it after all, begins to say if God will do that for her surely He'll do it for me and before it's over with it's screaming "I'm not going to let this beat me!"

I love giving my testimony! They said I wasn't leaving unless it was in a body bag! They said I'd be back!

Jokes on them, because here I am baby!

Update: Now is a good time to plug my book. It's on Amazon. It's titled, "The Adventures Of Sparky Madness And How She Met Captain Save A Hoe." You can just type Darlene Gossett into the search bar.

It's the story of my life. I never saw it coming, just like this book.

I just have to tell somebody.

My voice can never be silenced, about anything. Hahahaha.

It's available on Kindle.

I look back at what I wrote and it's painful, it's ridiculous, I can't believe this is who I was.

Can you imagine how relieved my family must be?

I gushed about god all the time, there was nothing I didn't give him credit for.

I gave this chick too much credit, she's back in the streets and has been for a while now.

I have a habit of doing that, giving people too much credit, knowing they are just people and they are going to disappoint me.

I'm learning to bet on myself, to invite myself, to show up just for me and no one else.

Seasons

Everything in life has seasons and mine just happen to be longer in the between than others. I've been a writer my entire life, I'm still writing, I've probably got ten books in me, but it's just not there. Sure I make my Facebook posts and I have my blog, but to sit down and write an entire book, not happening right now, but I do so hope it comes back soon.

My life is growing in excitement and wonder every single day. The most amazing things happen to me, around me, to people I come into contact with and I know that's God.

I'm painting again. It's been a minute. The stuff has been here waiting, it just hasn't flowed from me with the willingness it takes to produce the art. It's actually a very expensive hobby at this point, but I don't care, I sell some, I give some away, I paint paint paint when it's in me.

Right now, it's in me, the desire and hunger to paint.

There's a freedom in it I've never had before, this time. A freedom from fear, freedom from mistakes and my patience is growing in the details. I've got so much going on in my heart, it's flowing like a river out of me, along with this great joy I feel at being alive, at being loved, at having purpose and something other people need.

I never have been a selfish person, not even in the street, I have to give all of myself or I don't give.

I know what's happening to me right this minute is something bigger than I've ever hoped for, it's not going to end anytime soon and whatever comes of it, I'm at peace, I am enjoying myself, I am producing art, my art.

When I first began to paint again, I had this scene in my mind of an art show, canvas after canvas of my art work, on display, for sale, the work of my hands. I can still see that picture, but now the stock pile has grown even more and more are on the way and I'm loving it!

Everyone wants their moment in the sun, their time to shine, their fifteen minutes of fame, I'd be lying if I didn't have those desires. All that is fine and good but when it's for something so much bigger than yourself and for a purpose you didn't see coming when you first started, well that's a feeling that causes your feet to barely touch the ground, your heart to soar and your dreams to get bigger and bigger.

I don't even have a count right this minute for all the paintings I've managed to pull out of me. I want them to do great things. Isn't that crazy? I want my paintings to do great things, like bring happiness to people, to remind them of me every single day, to give them the same joy it gave me to paint them.

I want them to put huge wads of cash in my pockets, so I can buy more paint supplies, hahahahaha.

Still it's a season and we never know what God is planning for us.

I am a blessed woman, I love to paint, I love Jesus and I'm so excited for what's on the way.

Update: Finished that first book, working on some more stuff.

Still want those wads of money.

Apparantly God doesn't have a plan.

I have the plan, no god necessary.

Nothing was on the way except my awakening, my learning more than I'd ever learned before.

.

My Wedding

There are days I wake up and cannot for the life of me understand why I am so blessed. What makes me so special? Nothing at all. It's just that I have a heavenly Father who loves and cherishes me and puts the best of everything into my life! I am broken and flawed and as imperfect as a person can be, but He does not deny me His love. I am a hot mess five out of seven days a week and still He showers me with blessings. It is all to His glory what just happened to me, the day I was blessed with, the love I was shown by others. It was totally and completely God showing up and showing off like He always likes to do. It was all those times He puts the sky up for me and I let Him know how wonderful and beautiful it is and I thank Him knowing it's there just for me, even though the rest of the world can see it too.

I had no idea what God would do when I decided we should renew our vows. We'd just come from a lovely wedding our friends had New Year's Eve and now that I think about it, we totally forgot to wish one another a Happy New Year and kiss and I feel sure we were already in the bed asleep when the clock struck midnight. I made the event a couple of days later and then God began to grow it. It grew and grew until I thought I would die of happiness before the big day arrived.

Blessing after blessing poured in, in ways I've never experienced before.

I love to give, to do, to be a blessing to other people and I mean it when I say I never expect anything back.

Over the three months it took for the time to pass, God blessed me through his people and taught me to graciously accept those blessings. I really think He was putting me a place where I wouldn't cry the entire day, although I did cry and cry and cry for nearly a month preceding it. This totally amused my husband and he began calling me Crybaby.

I have a new found respect for wedding planners, photographers and those who make this sort of thing their living.

My girls threw me the most amazing party, to try on wedding dresses, their wedding dresses and it was so much fun!! The pictures were amazing and what bride wouldn't love a photo album wearing different wedding dresses? I had in fact set my heart on a dress, a dress I drove two hundred miles to get, a dress that my friend Robyn wore when she got married. I didn't know it was the dress until ***** helped me put it on and it fit like it was made for me. In that moment a joy welled up in my heart I couldn't explain and I told Robyn I just had to wear her dress.

She and I have been friends since the 8th grade and had not seen each other since 1986 until the summer before last. I've only seen her twice since then, once for less than half an hour, but I love her and she is my friend and we talk pretty regularly over Facebook and have had phone calls over the last year.

I sat in front of the computer too long, on Sunday, listening to music, just goofing off. My husband left for church and I was left to get ready for our vow renewal. Then, ***** and ***** and ******* showed up and got me ready, hair, temporary tattoos and

I'm so thankful ******* was busy fixing my hair at the time because they ended up on my left arm instead of my right and that made them in the perfect place for the pictures. ***** helped me get into the dress and *******'s two little girls, who were standing off to the side said "Wow." at the same time. I knew I'd made the right choice all along, but that moment sealed the deal.

His family was running late, we were in a crunch for time, we live streamed the service so we would know the exact moment they were finished.

They put me in the truck and wisked me off to the bar. It was a beautiful day, just another sweet touch God placed on a day so important to us and the restoration of our marriage.

They parked near where my brother was parked, on the side of the building toward the backside of the parking lot and he went in without even saying hi, but that's fine he was here for me.

I sat in the truck waiting for them to come and get me, beginning to worry about sweating, because of my make up. LOL. We all have this worry at one time or another.

They came running out to get me and help me around to the door.

N was in the parking lot, my ex daughter in law's fiance and he voiced his appreciation.

Standing at the front door, hearing my friend ******* sing, I just happened to catch a glimpse of Robyn's beautiful daughter, Amara and that moment in time will be forever captured because ***** took a picture of me as I was exclaiming, "She lied to me!" So there I am, standing in my girlfriend's dress, waiting to go in and marry my husband again. I was and still am the happiest woman in the world.

As I walked in to the bar, everyone cheered and whooped me in. I cannot describe what that felt like.

I don't know if I was shaking from nervousness or vibrating with excitement, but I took my husband's hand and stood there trying not to cry.

I stole a glance out over the crowd and my heart burst open with love at all the smiling faces of those who loved us, who came to show their support for us, to be a part of something so special in our lives.

His family came in while we were having our first dance, but mama wanted to hear our vows when we got back to our house, so we did them for her.

It was the best day of my life!!!! I married the man of my dreams again!!

Update: This is when I had friends. Well, you know what I mean. Anyway, it was glorious, it was another dumb decision I made on his part, it was the beginning of the end. He took the $500 that was gifted to us plus $200 more in overdrafts and relapsed.

It was my day and that's all that matters. They showed up for me that time, for sure.

I'm divorced now. It's a beautiful thing. I'm experiencing freedom I've never had before, happiness I never knew could be had and I don't miss him. What's to miss?

He overdrew my bank account over seven hundred dollars the last time.

On My Own

I have a whole new life, all new dreams, plans, a new job and nothing about my old life remains.

No one talks to me about religion except people on the internet. I have a few precious friends who still love me and don't make it weird for me. One lady has supported me and my dream of farming all this year. She's a devout christian and never talks about god to me. Her love for me is moving, because I'm sure she knows I'm a heathen.

I don't discuss religion on my page any longer, it's not worth the nonsense that comes back because of it. I don't want to hurt and or offend those I love. Some people just don't understand and there is nothing I can do to help them.

It's better to let sleeping dogs lie. There's enough people talking about religion, my voice does not need to be added to their numbers, it's not important to me anymore. I have no desire to change anyone's mind and or teach them anything. I'm only writing this book at the request of my friend and I wrote it along while back, finishing it for publishing and consumption.

People believe what they want to believe, there's no changing their minds when they are convinced. It's not something I find important any longer.

I stay off social media a great deal, nothing but politics and religion there most days. It's an old worn out argument and everyone seems to be spoiling for a fight. I post things and whoever communicates with me, or responds to me, those are the people I follow and talk with and respond to.

I belong to all sorts of groups where they are still hashing it out when I put that stuff to rest a long while ago.

I don't want to talk about it anymore, I don't want to see it anymore, I wish it would all go away, but that's not happening anytime soon.

This new life feels like I'm being rewarded.

God's Love Is Inclusive

For just a moment I want you to open your mind, clear all pre-conceived notions, all judgment, everything you've ever been taught, just sweep it all away. Drop your fighting stance, hold on to your pounce and save your argument. Take a deep breath and exhale. Imagine this is Jesus in the boat and you are the person going under. Jesus didn't ask you a single question about yourself, He just said, "I love you, I want to save you, do you believe me?" all in the moment of a heart beat. God does not pick and choose, He already chose and those are who would believe. We've all got issues, we've all got stuff wrong with us, we are messed up! He simply said "If they will believe I will save them.". Since God's love is inclusive, this includes all people. Drunks, thieves, prostitutes, drug dealers, adulterers, liars, slanderers, those who covet, murderers, drug addicts, pimps, gangsters and gay people. If I left anyone out it includes them as well. Love wins people. Belief saves. God fixes the stuff. Jesus stands in the gap for us. We have got to do better. He said love me and love them. If you really love him you automatically love them.

Update: Extreme study of biblical meaning has unveiled the god of the bible is one jacked up character and we are not even the audience.

Think about it. If someone could write a book intended for an audience that would live over two thousand years later, more people would have done it.

It's not a magic book. It's a horror story really, but they swoop in with grace and explain away the bi-polar behavior.

Their human sacrifice took care of that.

Is it possible people could have viewed it as myth, even then and that's why Constantine destroyed so much of the church's evidence?

One of the scholars, a historian, says they would make up background stories and families for mythical characters in those times. He has lots of degrees, I believe the things he says. He's spent a great deal more time looking at and taking it apart than I have. I don't have any titles or degrees.

I'm a myth camp atheist. I believe it's all myth and that camp stands right with me, but I don't believe any god lives anywhere outside of a book.

I tell people I'm a god just to be annoying.

I really enrages the religious ones.

There I've said it, that ugly word christians say with fear and venom. Atheist.

No reason to believe in a god.

Who said one existed in the first place?

As time has progressed I like the term heathen better and that's what I've labeled myself, without owing anyone an explanation for it.

Closing That Chapter

Unlike times in the past, I'm not lonely, I don't feel as if half of me is missing and I'm not jealous of others who have relationships.

He's been gone since, April, will be gone for the rest of my life and I don't even miss him.

What's to miss?

Money going to the dope man, everything that's not nailed down going to the dope man, the vehicles in the shop because they've been so abused and me digging myself out of a financial hole to fix everything that's gone down. There's nothing to miss.

For the first time in fifteen years I'm whole again. I sleep well at night, I cherish not having to hide things and being able to go to bed without worrying where my pocket book and my keys are.

It's heaven I tell you.

Your mate is supposed to be of help, comfort and support, not a never ending nightmare of the same old thing.

I stepped off the hamster wheel.

There are those who are nay sayers, who don't believe, who will say the silliest stuff to me, but I don't care, I don't have to prove anything to anyone and it's really none of their business.

He's gone, that's that, good day to you.

It's peaceful.

I don't have to spend money on anyone but the baby and me.

Unless you've been through it you can't imagine what it's like to live with an addict.

Everyday you try to empower them, to trust them a little bit, to put things right again. You're always working toward this goal you will never reach because they are going to do it again. You live your life with this dark cloud over your head just waiting for the moment it releases the storm you know is coming.

It's terrible! It's full of hurt and disappointment and being used knowing you let them do it. There's no hope for the future in it because the future is them getting high and it costing you everything.

I stood by him, I stayed down for him, I gave him more chances than he deserved and he still did the same exact thing over and over again.

No one can say a word about me, because I gave it my all, I gave him my all, it costed me more than anyone will ever know.

It's more than a car. I bought the car to keep him from stealing the truck and praise God it worked! The car is a seed to something better. Who cares about the car? I actually took it off my insurance and changed insurance companies because they didn't even want to cover the car because he was on the policy. I don't care about the car anymore, it served it's purpose. I'll pay it off, I'll get something else, or maybe I won't.

Who knows what God has in store for me, but one thing is for sure, it's not that.

Someone even had the nerve to say to me I would let him come back. Don't you know I saw blood?

No, I will not let him come back, he can't ever come back and it was his choice to leave in the first place. I didn't run him off, he made that decision on his own. Getting high has always been more important than me, than our marriage, than anything in the world for him, so I think it's safe to say he got what he wanted and I paid for it.

I'm not even mad.

I went to see what could be done about the car, called the police, sat with the baby screaming in the truck for over an hour, counting police cars as they drove past me.

They didn't do anything right and it didn't go down the way I needed it to, so who cares. They were calling me when I was getting on the expressway to come back home and that's the moment it didn't matter to me anymore.

He didn't say, "Hi, how are you doing?", the first words out of his mouth were, "Did you bring my stuff?", "Have you got a cigarette?", "I need some money."

I had been talking to God for over a week about how I didn't want to see him and I needed things to go peacefully and quickly so I could return home.

When I saw him running through the yards, it scared me so bad I forgot I was on the telephone with someone until they spoke to me again.

He's a shell of a man. He weighed 222 pounds when he left here, he probably weighs 160 now, his face is starting to cave, his arms don't have muscles anymore, his waist is probably 26 inches and had I not known his body language I never would have known it was him. He was sweating, wearing this hideous sweater I'd come to hate, wiping his face with it again and again, his mouth twitching, his eyes darting everywhere. He was digging around on the back of my truck, I already had it in reverse planning the moment I could escape, because the visit would only go down hill from there.

He said the craziest thing I ever heard to me.

"You left the dogs home by themselves?"

That question struck more fear in my heart than the fact he was standing there, high, dirty, looking crazy.

Apparently his mother isn't letting him live in her house anymore, because he keeps stealing from her.

I waited until he walked into her house to take my foot off the brake and leave, because I knew if I tried to back up and leave with him anywhere else he would be on the truck before I hit the street.

It was like watching a zombie circle around the truck, then he was in the passenger window, talking to the baby, who probably no longer knows who he is because he doesn't even look like the same person.

My legs were shaking, my heart was pounding in my throat and I felt sick to my stomach.

I never looked back, I just kept going. I drove home, forgot everyone else I was supposed to see, had to call someone who was supposed to come meet me, just kept going until the truck stopped in front of my house.

The love affair had ended the afternoon I woke up from a nap to find the car gone. My truck was in the shop because of his shenanigans and he'd taken money out of my desk, money that belonged to the company I work for. I forgave him the first time, but that was the boundary from then on.

I'm not sad like I've been in the past. My heart doesn't feel sorry for him anymore and it doesn't long to have him back either. Praise God.
I remember always being so sad that my "baby" was in the streets, poor poor hubby.

No!

He made the choice, he always chose that over me and it's not sad any longer. It's pathetic. It's like choosing an old, should've been thrown out hamburger from a fast food joint, over a cooked to order steak in a nice restaurant.

It's not sad anymore and I'm not sad he made it.

It was his decision.

The car you ask? It's not worth having, passenger mirror hanging off, bumper hanging off, trunk busted, windows busted out of the driver's side, flat tire, who knows what else. That car will sit there just like it is until the city makes them haul it off, it will never run again.

I'm left to pay it off, along with all the other stuff and when that's over with, what a relief it will be.

I'm already free. A divorce is inevitable and looked forward to. The papers are already filled out, they just have to be signed, notarized and filed. That's another $224 it never costed him.

There's no nagging fear in the back of my mind that he might show up, because he's not going anywhere, he's so stuck his feet might as well be in concrete blocks.

Those boys he thinks are his friends are watching him die and accepting every dollar he brings them. He's just another j to them.

Does God still love him? Of course He does. He's been sparing his life all this time, he's been hit by a bus, he's been hit by a car, he almost lost his foot and his life when that happened, he's been shot five times and he's still here.

Do I still love him?

No.

It's over. It probably shouldn't have happened, it was all me being a love sick girl, wanting something that wasn't good for me.

I am so relieved.

Update: This is the same exact way I feel today, to the letter. Same situation. Same things going on. Do you see a pattern here?

You Should Know

Today, in church, George was talking about how we need to call folks, how we shouldn't depend on others to see what we put on Facebook, when we are going through things. How we need to connect with others and let them know what's really going on with us. It was profound, hearing that, knowing what I've gone through this last week.

I didn't want to talk about it, but I found myself up in the middle of the night, falling to pieces, having cried for days, recognizing a ghost from my past.

For those of you who don't know, because I've never really discussed it openly, I have been mentally ill in my life, extremely, destructively, disastrously mentally ill. Going to the doctor, laying on the couch, being doped to the gills, labeled, categorized, diagnosed, give the girl a check mentally ill.

Even now it's so painful to even mention.

There's a stigma so dark attached to it, I've only trusted certain people to know.

I spent days crying and somewhere in all of that I realized, "This is more than just getting my heart broke and being rejected.", "This is more than the usual weeping I experience.", "This is more than disappointment and being exhausted and frustration, this is something totally different."

Damn!!!!!!

I remember feeling like this another time.

Damn! Damn! Damn! I thought this thing had gone away!

I thought I'd managed to get past this!

I hate the labels, the diagnosis, the categorization and the medicine.

I hate the way people tip toe around you and treat you with kid gloves and seem to be waiting for you to flip the hell out and go crazy.

It's not who I am, it's not my identity, it's not something I embrace or accept as being a part of me.

You'll hear me say things like, "They say this is what I have.", "This is what they've diagnosed me with.", "This is what they say is wrong with me."

It has to be something wrong with me right? Not everyone is certifiable crazy.

I don't have a problem with the word crazy, it's all the scientific crap they try to blow past me that bothers me.

Extreme bi-polar disorder, manic depressive with dis associative features. Dis associative features, it's not a freaking movie set!

I'm deeply disturbed this is happening! I'm even more disturbed at my urge to share it and put it out there for the whole world to see, but not nearly as disturbed as I was when a voice came along and started talking to me about ending it all.

It's such a long, horrific and tragic story, I don't want to go into the details.

It cost me everything, a marriage, my children, my freedom, and then some.

It sent me in a downward spiral that took me ten or more years to dig my way out.

It had me paying people who didn't give a crap about me or what happened to me, to listen and not help me solve my problems. It had me taking so much of a drug I should be dead because even the psychiatrist was a quack. It had me in a lot of deep dark places, doing really stupid and destructive stuff, it had me out of control.

Man oh man!

I keep seeing Jack Nicholson in The Shining with a hatchet busting the bathroom door, then saying "Here's Johnny."

Then comes Randy Quaid, the drunken pilot in Independence Day, flying into the space ship yelling, "Hello boys, I'm back!"

There are so many things playing out in my mind right this minute it would be impossible to describe them to you in a way that makes sense.

I don't have to accept it but I do have to own it, because I don't want to die.

I'm mentally ill.

There goes half the people I thought loved me and were my friends. Bye. It was nice knowing you.

I'm mentally ill.

There goes 90% of the men who may have wanted to date me. See ya fellas, those others chicks you are chasing don't look real stable either.

I'm mentally ill.

There goes anyone else who wasn't true to start with. What ever. Bye Felicia. Later.

Why am I telling you this?

I don't want to die!

I kept hearing another member's sermon where he talked about the spirit of suicide coming on him, a great man of God, how it began to lie to him and tell him how no one would care, how easy it could be.

I don't want to waste away in this desert of emotions.

I don't want everyone being unaware of what's happening to me, because it is happening to me, it's not something I'm doing to myself.

I hate it, my heart is broken, my mind is in a million places and my emotions, they are locked in the trunk and driving at the same time, which is never ever a good thing.

No one can look at me and say, "Get your shit together Darlene.", because no one has the answers as to how that will actually be done.

I thought I did have it together!

I haven't felt this way in more than twenty years!

Why did it come back?

Did it not ever go away?

What in the heck is going on here?

I'm sure I'm not the only one. I'm sure there are others just like me, who live in the shadows, don't want to talk with others about it, carry a certain shame about it.

Right this minute, I am the only one, the most important one and I'm telling you, I am suffering from mental illness.

There I said it!

Damn!

I'm trying to set something up so I can talk with someone, start trying to dig back into the root of the problem, find answers for something that will never be concrete and get through the next moment.

So why are you telling me this Darlene?

I don't know!

I need your help! I need your love! You don't have to understand me, just accept and love me! I'm an open book, I'm not trying to hide anything from anyone and furthermore I can't afford to because this monster is so much bigger than I am to begin with.

I'm broken.

Now you know my deepest darkest secret, I don't know what I expect you to do with it, I'm just trying to get everything out in the open, release stuff I don't need and let people know what's going on with me. I can't front and fake it anymore, it's not going to let me anyway. You're liable to see crazy stuff that defies explanation, I hope you don't but it could happen.

I can't shut myself off, isolate from everyone and hide it, because it's there. It's the elephant in the room and it has to be talked about.

I'm going to copy and paste some information I found, simply because people need answers, hell I need answers. If you have information you can share with me, encouragement, stories of your own, that would be great and probably help.

I've used every ounce of courage I had, I'm completely vulnerable and at the mercy of the world right this second and that's all I'm going to say about it, for now.

Being mentally ill means:

Thinking outside of "normal" rational concepts, causing you not to participate in a normal life.

For a portion of one's life, it is the inability to make one's own choices based on what makes the most sense to them.

Possibly thinking self-destructive thoughts or do things that are self-destructive.

Sometimes having an inability to understand what people are saying to you and are not able to control your own behavior.

Having others be exasperated with you or treating you like a child.

Often not understanding the motivation for one's own deeds or speech.

Constantly regretting one's actions, but not knowing what to do about it.

Blaming others and your environment for your own feelings and difficulties because you don't know who else to blame.

Assuming what others are thinking, and often misunderstanding other's motives.

Being mentally ill does not mean:

That a person is irrational, but that their thinking involves a different kind of rationality.

That a person is violent, except in rare cases.

That a person has a lesser intelligence.

That a person cannot function normally in life, although they may need some special assistance or allowances.

Update: I don't know what the hell was happening here but I really needed to get a grip and smoke some weed or something.

I waited on god, prayed, begged, and kept going day after day, never holding him accountable for not showing up.

I heard the same lame played out comments over and over again. People really don't think about what they are saying.

I've been told stuff so dumb I didn't even respond, other stuff I wanted to go through the computer and beat the other person senseless.

You'd be surprised how many people have never questioned their beliefs, the god they think they believe in and or their faith.

I began looking at religions and gods across the board and that one thing ended all of it for me. If there are all these millions of gods, many of them long before the christian god. Dying and rising gods can be found across many religions, all of them with a similar back story. The first one was female.

Go and find out for yourself.

Normal

It's safe to say I've never been normal. LOL. It's just a label we stick on things, like the
labels we stick on everything else. I can appreciate things needing description but
we've gone way over the edge with the labeling of everything.

We're all uniquely, fearfully and wonderfully made.

We're children of God, how does this happen to us?

I don't have any answers but when I do you can bet I'm going to shout them from the
rooftops, I'm going to help anyone I can with what I've learned and I'm going to be well
again and much longer this time.

I've reached out to someone I trust and she's coming to my house tomorrow after she
gets out of class. She's still going to school, has been going to school almost the entire
time I've known her and I trust her with my heart and what we will talk about.

Who knows? I might end up being her thesis. I might end up being her first success
story. I might end up finding out things about myself I don't know.

I don't know what's going to happen anymore than the next person does, but I'm not
going to let this destroy my life again. I'm not going to fall into this like I would the
arms of a lover and let it embrace me. I'm not going to deal with this the way I did in
the past either.

My sister called today to check on me. She was the first person I said it out loud to.
 "I'm pretty sure I'm sick again sis." You can't imagine how crazy that sounds to me,
knowing who I am and who I belong to. Jesus is not mentally ill, so how do I walk

through as He is, so am I in this world, knowing this is something I can't ignore.

Ignoring it won't make it go away.

Its these things that don't line up with scripture, with the journey, that completely contradict our identity.

More questions, even less answers.

Grrrrrrrr.

Just for today, I'm okay.

Praise God.

Update: So the questions began.

I was just fine, going through some normal stuff.

I broke up with god and religion, so that was traumatic.

My ex is a tornado in my life.

I stay pretty grounded and haven't been medicated in over twenty years.

I learned a lot about the things they labeled me with and I've lived past that part of my life now.

Everyone has emotions, a little depression here and there, loneliness, feeling a little off. It happens to all of us, life is not easy.

She and I came to the conclusion I was just fine and it was good that I reached out either way, because she learned something.

I am pretty steady most of the time. I have my moments where I cry, where I'm super emotional but I think some of that is just being a woman.

I choose to be happy.

I choose to live life right in front of me.

I choose to do all the things that make me happy.

I choose to continue to dream, though none have really ever come true.

It's really sad when you think about it. None of my dreams have come true.

I would say things like, "Okay God, I'm counting on you to pull a miracle off today.",

or, "Can we have a better showing than the last time?"

I wanted to get all the spiritual leadership, concerned citizens, people who were willing

to go out into the community to create change. My girl made me a super nice flyer. I

advertised it everywhere I could on social media, my page, groups, yard sale sites. I

advertised it for a long while. I talked to people I knew. They said things like, "Just tell

me where and when, I'll be there."

The morning of the breakfast we were supposed to meet for at Gold Corral, I didn't even

have the money to eat.

My neighbor showed up.

It seems like everything I believed god for exceeded his ability to help me out, so it

would be better or it would grow.

I followed her back to her house, she got a call and ditched me immediately.

I went home defeated, as usual.

Why didn't anyone show up?

Everyone always talks about how they want to do things, to make the world better, their communities better, something for someone less fortunate.

Oh but that requires showing up sweety.

That requires effort and sticking to something.

People are like butterflies they flit from one project to the next.

They are easily distracted and if they aren't 100% comitted, they will not hang around for long. They'll show up a few times and not participate, stand around watching everyone else, then they'll stop showing up altogether.

I don't beg people and I don't pet anyone but my dog.

You want to do it or you don't.

I am explosive at setting things up, the problem is no one ever shows up to see my handiwork.

I found a way into the entire Mary Kay corporation and keep getting blown off.

I'm not like everyone else.

I don't want to be like everyone else.

My mother struggled with me my entire childhood because of this one character traight.

I don't want to look like the other girls, to dress like the other girls, I want to look and dress like me. I don't spend my time comparing myself to anyone, because I can't find anyone to compare myself to.

If that sounds arrogant, then you just don't know me.

I love people, I'm a compulsive hugger, I'll do anything in the world for you.

Whatever It Is It's Just Visiting, It Will Pass. Wow.

I love that!

Whatever it is it's passing.

Storms are passing over, they never last.

Whatever it is you are going through it's just something that's visiting.

Breathe.

Be encouraged you're not the only one.

It's okay to cry, to rant, to scream at the walls, sometimes you have to do that. It's okay to fall completely apart and go off the deep end, but get back up!

Move on from that moment.

It's okay, but let's keep living.

Own it but don't live in it.

God has a purpose for your life and nothing can change that. Stand up, brush yourself off, wipe the tears off your face and take a deep breath.

Just breathe.

I can see my spirit eyes closed, small smile, taking a deep breath.

Exhaling.

We all have moments.

That's exactly what it is a moment and some last longer than others.

I understand you're hurting, you can't help it, it's happening to me too.

Let's keep moving, search for the happiness and the beauty of it all and keep walking this thing out, because giving up and surrendering is not an option.

Breathe.

This too shall pass.

Update: Life is painful at times. There's no need going around in denial about it. You have to face each and every day head on. You have to choose your battles and fight them.

Most of the time we're only fighting ourselves and our own thoughts.

A month after I had him home I asked myself what the hell was I thinking. Why do I keep doing these things to myself?

I started meditating and listening to the art of mindfulness. I chose to be happy.

He once said, "you're crazy as hell."

Me: I wasn't like this before you met me. You are the reason I'm crazy like this.. You have no one to blame but yourself for this crazy. I'm not like this when you aren't around either.

I didn't criticize him. I waited on him like he was a guest. I let him have his space and his choice was to sneak and lie, again.

Do we know the definition of insanity yet kids?

He wanted to leave, he just wasn't man enough to come out and say it.

I'm Gonna Change The World!!!

Believe it!

I'm screaming God send me and He sends me and I go!

All you have to do is sit back and watch.

My Father is the creator of the universe and He loves the wild ones. I just happen to be one of those and yes I'm crazy enough to stand on 3,657 promises He's made me, to stand on truth and to believe I'm gonna change the world.

Update: I still want to change the world.

I want to help end racism.

I want to completely annialate human trafficking and pedophelia.

I don't want people going hungry.

I hate that children die every day.

I thought god was supposed to love us all.

I thought he was in control.

I thought he was going to work things out.

What kind of god allows those things to happen to those he loves?

What kind of god lets people buy and sell one another if they are all supposed to belong to him?

What kind of god would watch a child literally starve to death when there's enough food in the world?

Seems to me everybody's god would, doesn't matter what you call it.

Religious people turn their noses up at those who really need help. They shun one another, they turn on each other quicker than wolves in packs.

Don't get it twisted and say that I'm saying all religious people are like this, but the vasts majority can pass the test.

I've had a great deal of experience with religious people. I'm not over exagerating or making claims I can't back up. Truth is a curse for me. A lie doesn't care who tells it as long as it gets told. I'd rather tell the truth either way.

Religion holds no truth.

Morals and ethics are not taught in religion.

Gods are jealous and destructive beings, according to the stories. I can't say I've blamed a thunder storm on a god. Although, they do say Thor is the god of thunder.

See how that works?

I Love The Underdog!

un·der·dog

ˈəndərˌdôg/

noun

a competitor thought to have little chance of winning a fight or contest.

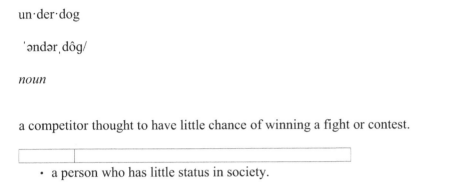

- a person who has little status in society.

I'm that person who feels bad for the losing team.

I'm that person who stands up to bullies for others.

I'm that person who is always going to stand for and root for the underdog.

God had to make me this way, because most people really don't care.

The world at large wants to see others lose, but me, I want to see everyone win. I want

to see everyone reach their dreams.

I have no problem with others around me doing better than I am. I like to cheer

everyone on.

They inspire me, they challenge me to do better, to do more, to be more.

I'm no hater and never have been.

A warrior fights for those who aren't able to fight for themselves. A warrior protects the

lives and hearts of others.

war·ri·or

ˈwôrēər/

noun

1.

   (especially in former times) a brave or experienced soldier or fighter

Love never ever hurts others.

There's so much madness in the world, people being mean to one another, tearing one another apart, standing by and videoing others being hurt.

It breaks my heart.

There was a time when I apologized to all the people I used to go to school with. My memory isn't that great because of the damage I've done to myself using drugs and there was this lie in my spirit that I'd been mean to others without cause. Every single one of those people came back to me and told me stories where I protected them, where I stood up to the bully for them, where I righted a wrong for them.

I was amazed.

The same thing happened in the clubs. They used to tell stories about me I couldn't believe, because I drank so bad I couldn't remember. I asked them why they even liked me or talked to me and every one of their responses were, "You never were mean to me, you took care of the person who was being mean."

Loving people makes you want to protect them, to guard them from harm. It makes you want to be kind to them, to do for them, to protect them from anyone who thinks otherwise.

When I stand before my Father, I'd rather find out I've been wrong about everything I've ever believed, than for Him to know I purposely hurt someone in His name.

I am a warrior and I love the underdog.

Update: I still love the underdog. I've been the underdog most of my life.

I no longer believe I'll be standing in front of anyone at the end of my life. I believe, metaphorical writings don't magically become real places.

I am not a turn the other cheek sort of girl and that's not my imaginary friend anymore. You come at me, I'm coming right back.

I'm not a doormat for christian and religious folks any longer. You're not gonna just run your mouth at me, giving no thought to the things you are saying. I don't care what you believe, you will not inflict your religious crap on me.

Do you know where you're going if you die tonight?

What kind of dumb ass question is that?

If I die tonight I'm going to the coronor's office you idiot?

If I'm dead why would I care?

Religion has had thousands of years to prove itself and still can do no better than wait until you're dead. 1-800-GET-A-GRIP.

Do you know where you are going if you don't get out my face with that mess?

If your god is so great and you're made in his image?

Why don't you act more like him?

Oh wait. You do act like him. He once got pissed off once and killed everybody, according to your holy book. You're always claiming to be fighting some kind of battle in the army of the lord.

Well, you see, your problem is you can't belong to the book club if you don't read the book and you've obviously not been reading the book, so we're going to have to revoke your membership and send you straight to hell now. Bye bye, have a nice day. Remember my god is a killer.

So many people are not completing the required reading and that's a huge problem. How are you going to argue about the bible with me if you've never read the whole thing and I've read it one hundred times?

My eye witnesses are alive and can testify to my having done so without being under threat of death. My eye witnesses can describe the book in question to you, it's been the same one for sixteen years. My eye witnesses are real and can read and write and they know to wash their behinds every day.

No one in my camp is running around destroying evidence so the word won't get out. Speaking of evidence, most of it I feel like are the same as election results, tampered with and twisted so much, no one will ever accept or really know the truth in the first place.

A god that can't write his own book?

Doesn't that make you even the least little bit suspicious?

Like this guy created the entire universe and can't create a book?

He needed some men to do it for him?

A god that killed everybody, then raped a virgin, then came as a baby and killed himself because his people are so awful.

Do you hear how crazy that sounds?

Don't say that's not what it says. We've clarified that I know exactly what it says.

How does a god that murders person after person represent love in any way, shape, form, or fashion in your mind?

How do you find love in, "I love you but if you don't love me back I'm going to burn you for eternity."?

Riddle me that religious folks.

I am god, if you don't love me I'll destroy you.

That dude sounds more like the man I'm trying to divorce rather than a god.

Shouldn't a god be more helpful.

Shouldn't there be something each god does that let's his people know he's there? Aside from their collective ignorance I mean.

Go and google scriptures where god is telling people to kill. Gee that guy looks like he really loves some folks to me.

Yeah, I can see why you would want to worship that guy.

Actually the book is their idol. They think it's a weapon, that it's this magical gateway to their god and a metaphorical kingdom that's been written about.

They've set it up for themselves and forced it on absolutely anyone who would take it.

They don't care about your questions and can't answer half of them.

You're going to be cussed out and insulted when the kindergarten understanding breaks down during the conversation.

You're going to get called names and if you're an atheist, they are going to go that further mile and treat you even worse: like you're shit on their shoes or something.

They assume that atheists are stupid, when it is completely the opposite, only a fool could believe it for long.

I've read plenty of books that were better.

Christianity could throw away the bible and use the Shack, that would make the world far better than the state it's in now.

They should also get off their asses and do something that's not motivated by this overwhelming need to be good.

I even caught myself once thinking, what would they think?

Who gives a shit what they would think?

They look like crazy people now.

You're not so crazy after all are you sister?

When you look at the book and see the story is over and it wasn't about you anyways, who cares, game over.

Why are we still talking about this dang book? Can we talk about my book? It's pretty damned interesting.

Invite The Misfits

I love the misfits, the one's standing on the outside looking in. The ones who feel left out because they aren't in the cool click. The ones willing to do something when no one else is. The ones whose hearts are so on fire and hungry for something, once they've got hold of it they'll never let go.

Invite the misfits.

That's the war cry of Renegades of Grace Ministries.

We are supposed to be united, one body, but unfortunately there are a lot of things in this world that are not as they should be.

I can't live a life of church and work and sleep, I've got to have more, I'm asking God for more. I want to do more, see more, and be more.

God has been growing my crew and man oh man they are really something else! They are dedicated, want to do anything and everything necessary and they are so much more than the cool click.

I love their hearts, their drive and that willingness. I need them and all the wonderful qualities they bring to the table. I need more souls like them because it's so much bigger than all of us.

For some reason showing up a disease for others, no matter how often you invite them, they aren't going to show up and they aren't going to invite you to their stuff either. It's alright, it's not a big deal. I'm not scared to stand alone and neither are any of them, because God makes us able to do all we do. Those who choose not to are the one's really missing out. You can't sleep on your purpose or you live a life unfulfilled.. If you won't show up for others you can't expect them to show up for you, although my bunch is gonna show up.

They've been shunned, they've been left out, they've been on the outside looking in and that's not always the most pleasant place to be.

No one wants to be left out.

We all want to belong to something, to know we are loved and valuable. God created us for community, so it completely makes sense to want to be a part of something.

There are those who will tell you they are too busy, they've got too much going on. We do too.

We've got children and jobs and bills and partners and all the same stuff going on as the ones who claim to be busy.

Willingness is the difference, laying down our lives for others is the difference. We don't want to live all bottled up in our neat little organized worlds, we want it all.

We are the ones chasing everything God has for us.

It's more than the lives we are living, it's kingdom.

Jesus loved those no one else wanted, no one else loved, those who were shunned, mistreated, looked down on. He loved them and He changed their lives forever.

Everyone He touched were healed and whole. He didn't turn anyone away, not ever.

He supped with them, His very presence they hungered for, needed, the great I am.

They were His people, the ones He came for.

I can see Him sitting there, hearing their conversations, seeing the smiles on their faces, the awe and wonder that He would love them. I can see them, the misfits. Dirty faces and hands, no clean changing of clothes, hurt and broken people who desperately needed His love.

We are those misfits.

I'm still in awe that He would love me. I'm still at that table supping, smiling, talking to those around me, enjoying the company and the meal and the presence of my Savior. I see all my people there, my Ride or Die's, smiling, talking, doing the same thing I'm doing.

Do you remember when you were broken and felt unloved?

Invite the misfits.

Update: They left as quickly as they came.

When you stop going to church people see no reason to support your causes.

I've been in church one Sunday. I had a moment to speak, asked everyone for help, so I could buy food to go to the streets. After I sat back down I heard a couple talking about how they'd been here and there and the wait staff as the restaurants they had been eating at were amazed they could afford to buy other people's food. Those same good christian people let me walk out of that church empty handed that day.

How you could even tell that story after what I just said without slapping some money in my hand?

That's when I started watching people, paying attention to who was real and who wasn't.

Who came to church when we had guests speakers.

Who didn't bother when our own pastor was out.

It's not important anymore. It is what it is.

Forgiveness And Being Honest With Yourself

Forgiveness is for you!

Holding on to things and hurts is a slow poison that kills your soul.

Everyone has been hurt, people have done dumb stuff to us, treated us as if we were less than, hurt us to our very cores.

There's been much talk about this lately.

I've been examining myself, places of hurt in my life, people who have hurt me and searching for places where I can extend forgiveness to others in my life.

Update: I can extend forgiveness but you don't get to play with me.

What is up with people projecting? I mean seriously? You don't know me, how the hell did you get that much information about in the simple question I asked, "which god?"

They try to shrink you, they say things about you that are completely untrue. They just run on and on like a freight train with no brakes.

Their problem is they have forgotten they can get their ass beat. They've forgotten there are people who the world who don't give a crap about your god or your little book and if you were brave enough to say that to my face, well, you see what had happened was.

Think of all the people straight up murdered because they wouldn't convert or pledge allegiance to some imaginary god.

Think of the ones in the world today. Killing other people over imaginary stuff. Get a grip people.

End times.

End times came and went.

The rapture was the dream of some little girl in the 1800's.

There is no hell and that should give you a real fat clue there is no heaven and if you're living your life here to get somewhere else, well I'm sorry sweety but the rest of us think you're a stupid ass. Oh yeah and you better do something about that nasty attitude before you don't get to go.

Your god could change his mind and burn you for eternity.

Now take all that stuff you just said to me, that you couldn't possibly know, pack up your imaginary friends and your book you think so much of and move it down the road sister, we're all sold out of crazy here.

Thank you and have a nice day.

And remember Jesus loves you.

Not Getting Tazed Is Pretty Cool

Seize today like a child and a crazy looking dog that have just made a discovery, that will change their lives forever. All things work for your good and God has a plan for you. You're not stuck, you can't even begin to mess it up until your Daddy doesn't love you, you don't need anybody but Jesus and He ain't going nowhere. So breathe, step back, regroup, forgive, pray, move on and slay your giants Only have positive conversations with yourself and others. Look at the bright side in everything. For instance, I've had plenty of encounters with the police, only one of them bad, two I wanted to make bad, but I never got tazed. Praise God! I never got tazed, because I straightened my behind up and moved out of Alabama before they started tazing folks pretty regularly. My friend told me he's been tazed four times and its part of his job. Whatever that means? & That! Not happening, nope nope, not gonna do it. Be blessed Jesus loves you. Yes I acted a fool and got into some scrapes with the law, but I never got tazed and I think that totally kicks butt! Nothing can stop you, our God is an awesome God. All His answers are yes and amen for His children. He's a good good Father. You've got nothing to lose NOW GET IN THE PIT AND TRY TO LOVE SOMEONE!!!! RIDE OR DIE!!! WWB!!!

Update:

I know, it's kind of sickening.

I truly believed it.

I repeated all the good stuff I heard from others all the time, it's a game of parroting.

All you have to do is go back across decades of videos and see what's been said. Same

old hell fire and brimstone preaching. Same old you've got to love god guilt trip.

It's all the same, cookie cutter religion, they just keep softening the language of it.

They keep picking different hooks to say.

They keep focusing on the good parts, because dealing with the text is above the level of

religion.

Religion doesn't require you to think, you just have to look and talk and act like

everyone around you.

Praise the lawd.

Some days

"We look for visions of heaven and we never dream that ll the time God is in the commonplace things and people around us."

That's so deep! I want my heaven right here, right now, to get my face rocked by it!

Love wins!

Think about all the people who are in your heart.

All of them.

Do you have that picture?

That's your heaven.

Wowwwwwwwwww!

That's your heaven and there is love in that.

All the people you love, people who need answers to prayers, who need healing in their bodies, their minds and their hearts. People with issues just like you. People. Brothers and sisters. Everybody is the same to me, so sinners or saints in my life, only my brother and sisters. Our Daddy owns everything.

Love.

Instead of looking ahead, wishing for this, waiting on that, let's live in this moment right now and embrace the love we feel for everyone else and be.

Stop everything!

Breathe!

You have this moment in time, right here right now, to be love to someone else, to everyone else! Who cares who they are? Where they come from? What they did last night?

Love, pass it out!

For real!

Throw that stuff around!

That's the best stuff in the universe!

Love!

I'm a firm believer that heaven is not a place I'm trying to get to, I'm trying to be heaven in someone else's life every minute of every day. I'm ushering heaven in, to be lived in right this second!

All that love is your heaven!

The world can't touch you!

You don't have anything to do with what's going on in the world! It's not your business!

Your business is love!

Your business is kingdom business!

Your business is healing the sick, setting the captives free and raising the dead!

Ya heard me?

Your heaven is right in front of you, wrapped up in all of the people who you love.

To heal those broken places.

To hold them just a little tighter with each embrace.

To be the answer to their prayers.

To love them, most of all to love them!

I get to love on the most amazing and interestingly smelly people on the face of the planet!

My life is so good!

I don't care what was on the news! I never watch it! It's all lies!

My Daddy doesn't worry about all of that.

I'm going to sit here listening to this beautiful music in my Daddy's presence and keep living this beautiful life. It doesn't matter what's going on anywhere else.

There's no danger.

There's nothing to fear or worry about.

Exodus 14 14 God will fight the battle for you! And keeps your mouths shut!

The message says God will fight the battle for you. And you? Keep your mouths shut!

Wowwwwwwww.

I got this! Shut up!

Everyone of us have probably said that at one time or another.

I got this! Shut up!

Well alright then!

Nothing more to say.

Just sit back and watch my Daddy do His thang!

Love makes it alright.

Absolutely everything is right with the world when you're walking in love.

We were created for love.

I want to be love to everyone who meets me.

I have so much I can't stop giving it all away.

These folks that like to go around all gloom and doom, the world is coming to and end,

oh my gosh, oh my gosh.

How sad.

Peace is found in the Father.

No one can steal it from us.

There's nothing to worry about.

We know how it ends.

Love wins.

We are His kids, precious and cherished.

Heaven is right in front of me.

Whom shall I fear?

Perfect love casts out all fear and I am afraid of nothing.

It's so good you have to give it all away.

You aren't scared you might get hurt, or be misunderstood.

You aren't scared they won't love you back, you just give it without regard to what could

happen.

It's freely given, all of it, without fear or restraint.

Love.

I want to be beauty for someone's ashes.

I want to be healing in broken places.

Laughter for tears to someone.

I want to be that healing hug that changes absolutely everything!

I want people to accidentally brush against me in public and get healed from my clothes!

I want supernatural healing to take place in every building my body enters and walks

through!

I'm crazy enough to believe it!

That's love!

Love!

Nothing can separate us from that love!

Now get in the pit and try to love someone!

Getting Told All About Yourself

What's the deal with this?

I told someone they hurt me not too long ago and they told me all about myself.

How I rip people up on my page.

For the life of me I can't find that post.

How I'm supposed to be setting an example.

Ha!

Me setting an example?

Not happening.

I mean who cares my feelings were hurt?

Who cares it took courage to speak up.

Told me all about myself.

Don't watch me, because I know for a fact I'm not going to get something right, I'm going to go off the deep end or say something crazy, or do something that makes everyone cringe.

You're not supposed to be watching me, you're supposed to be watching Jesus.

So, apparently it's this thing to rip the brethren to shreds. When they say something biblically inaccurate, when they tell us they are hurt, when they do something we don't like, I guess for any reason.

I see it every single day.

When it happened to me I decided it was a good time to step back and take stock of the people in my life.

Who's really there for me?

Who really supports me and not just talks about supporting me.

Who gives me lip service and who really gives me their heart.

A lot of lip service goes on in our lives.

I can see hundreds of faces, all smiling, all I love you's and hugs, but how many of them are really there?

How many of them really mean what they are saying?

Maybe two dozen.

Maybe more, because I never really count them.

Always remember, nothing others do is because of you.

I know it's a tough one and we take everything so personally.

Nothing anyone else does is because of you.

They come at you crazy, say mean and cruel things, tell you all about yourself, but it's not because of you, it's their problem, it's what's going on with them.

You have nothing to do with it.

The second agreement says don't take anything personal. It's a hard thing to practice and I have to do it every day because people piss me off.

What's Your Good News?

Let's say you're standing in the pulpit, you've been asked to speak, you're all jacked up with excitement and nerves and all those faces staring back at you. All those faces! You're shaking, your stomach won't be still, you've got something to say.

The gospel is good news right?

What are you going to talk about?

Everyone is expecting good news, because the gospel is good news and they've been preaching the other way for entirely too long.

What if?

This is the only opportunity you are ever going to have in your entire life to say something to a group.

What can you say to them that will change their lives?

Think about it.

Is it good news?

When others hear it will their spirits dance around in happiness and confirmation?

This one chance!

Once in a lifetime opportunity.

Say something!

What are you going to say?

Love has a name.

Jesus.

What heals and makes whole?

LOVE!

JESUS!

What heals broken places in our lives?

Love!

Jesus!

That's good news!

Such good news!

I'm getting excited!

Good news is that moment when a soul stops and thinks, "Wow, I'm not the only one."

Good news is when someone exhales that sigh of relief because they aren't going to hell, their life before Jesus was hell!

Why would you waste a good message talking about nonsense that it the complete opposite of life?

Speak life!

Tell them how loved they are!

It's not a lie!

Tell them how nothing can separate us from His love!

It's okay we all don't believe the same, families argue, no two people believe exactly alike and freedom allows you to be in perfect union with Him.

You're in a relationship with Jesus!

What can you tell others about that?

What I believe and what my relationship looks like are two entirely different universes.

I love Jesus!

We're always chasing one another down with this love exchange. He woos me and pursues me, He is the lover of my soul.

He's not concerned with how I behave, what I've done, where I come from, He loves me right here, right now, in this very moment and He's never going to stop loving me for all of eternity.

Tell them!

That's good news!

Set them free to love the Father!

Tell them how amazing they are!

How loved they are!

Tell them they are more valuable than precious stones.

Everything works for their good!

Tell them all the good news of the kingdom!

The crier only calls out good news about the kingdom. He doesn't stand in the square whining about an approaching enemy, warning others of impending doom, yelling tales of woe to passersby, he's always proclaiming the goodness of the kingdom, the goodness of the king.

He is The King of Kings and The Lord of Lords.

He owns everything!

He's a good good Father!

His mercy endures forever!

What are you going to say to them?

You'll never hear me talk about darkness.

Love is my religion.

Love is good news.

Love wins!

Don't waste your one message babbling on and on about demons and hell and things we've obviously misunderstood, or translated wrong in some way.

You're a fisher of men!

You're winning souls, not scaring them away!

Good news is a hope and a future.

Everything works for your good.

God is never going to stop loving you.

What's your good news?

My good news is I'm still insane, just not indoctrinated anymore. I've recently had a great deal of mental illness, but it's nothing new and I recognize it for what it is. I'm doing well, learning to live alone.

Do It Just Once! You'll Never Be The Same

I just got home from Lover's Lane. What is Lover's Lane you ask?

Lover's Lane is looking like Jesus in service to others.

Today we did something different.

If you know anything about us, we take home cooked meals to the streets every single

Sunday, cold water, socks, whatever anyone gives us to take.

There's a shelter for men down there, Friendship Mission. These are the guys

transitioning from the streets, getting shuffled around by the VA and trying to make it. I

can't even tell you how many times I've walked in there to simply say, "I love you.", to

the people who were there. I stop and tell them "I love them" all the time. If you gave

me a truck load of food tomorrow I would drive straight down there and give it to those

guys.

Today, it was cooking, cooking cooking. They have a huge kitchen, so we were all

together, Joe, Joseph, Sharon, Amber and later Amanda and Tammy.

We stood in that kitchen putting food together from two this afternoon until almost five

thirty. Hamburgers and hotdogs on the grill, coleslaw, mashed potatoes, potato salad,

baked beans bacon and brown sugared up, and three cakes, two lemon one chocolate.

 Those guys went crazy for that lemon cake! I loved it!

We all did something, it was a group effort. We cooked for probably 60 and fed our

usual 30-40.

One guy who is always way up the street saw me drive through earlier in the afternoon and came down there right before we were leaving to get some food. I told the others, they didn't show.

I was so full of joy and love I wasn't even hungry when I sat down to try to eat. I probably a one bite of everything just to see how it turned out.

I encourage you to find something to do, go somewhere and help cook, strike out on your own and do kind things for others. Laying our lives down for others is where it's at.

Your life will never be the same and you won't be the same either.

It's all for them, every moment of it, such a beautiful experience. Like getting to cook Christmas dinner for everyone you ever loved, every week. :)

You don't understand it unless you do it and when you do it, man oh man, the kingdom of heaven comes down!

People are in need, doesn't matter why they are in need. It's not hard to be love and give away from yourself, you just do it. You find ways to do it, you find places to go to do it and your heart is set to do it.

God took me out of a dark and desolate place and did the most beautiful thing to my heart making that same place beauty for my ashes.

Do it just once! Something! Anything! You'll never be the same!

It's always Jesus.

Just So You Know

Yes, I'm talking to my husband again, dang it.

We should go ahead and get that out of the way right now.

I know all the things I've said, I know the things I've purposed in my heart and I know the hell he's put me through.

Grace over looks those things, forgives and forgets and stays open to give love.

It had to be God that made me take the phone call because I've been blocking numbers and hanging up on him for over a year now.

It's gonna have to be God for everything else as well.

I'm exhausted. Sixteen years of madness.

We met in the streets, both of us full blown crack addicts, homeless, alone.

It's so dumb but I loved him the minute I laid eyes on him and didn't even know his name.

I've taken him back time and time again, gone through crazy stuff every single time, tried saving him for years.

Guess what? I can't save him!

Guess what else? I'm too tired to try anymore!

It would be so much easier if he weren't a nice guy, if I didn't love him, if I knew how to stop being his friend.

It's so crazy!

The day I preached about the $54,000 bottle of oil the woman at the Pharisee's house poured out on Jesus, eight years of letters stacked up on the podium in front of me, he called.

He's back in jail and says it was all God and I have no choice but to believe him because I know it's all God. Only God could have made me answer that call because I'd sworn to never talk to him again.

My divorce has been filed and paid for and for all I know I am divorced, but I don't have the heart to tell him because he was so dang happy to hear from me.

He says he's praying for restoration in our marriage.

Really? Seriously?

Knowing my Daddy and knowing what grace looks like, I already know the outcome, but two can play that game, so I am praying as well.

The one thing I've asked him to do he's never done.

For sixteen years I've asked him go somewhere and have plenty of places he could go. For sixteen years he's done it his way and not honored my request and his way does not work.

I've quit trying to understand or figure out the way he's addicted, because it's obviously different for each person and there are no clear answers to be had.

My statement to God was, "Lord if you'll let me be this man's wife, I'll do anything." Stupid girl!

You would not believe the things I've done.

Finally, he used that word!

I said to him, "You know you're going to Canaan Land right?"

"Yes,", he replied, "I will do anything to have my family back."

There's that word, anything. I will be forever cautious for the rest of my life about using that word..

It's the first time he's used it, LOL. He's about to find out what anything is.

No matter what it looks like from the outside looking in, over the years, time after time, we are in covenant with God, we are one flesh and one flesh cannot be separated which is why divorce has been so frowned upon in theology.

This is not the first but the second year we've been apart because I couldn't live with it anymore. My love is not unconditional, unfortunately.

Funny thing about that is anyone who comes along who might be someone I could possibly date, no dice. They never make it to even a first date. They quickly vanish into whatever their lives look like and I'm still sitting here all by myself. He recently revealed to me how He's saving my heart and someone else's, because I might have some difficult decisions to make in the very near future and if I were involved with someone that would make those decisions even more difficult and they would very likely get hurt.

My pastors are life coaching about marriage right now and there are so many more factors that come into play.

I'm saying this because I know there will be critics, there will be those who judge me, tell me I'm crazy, turn their backs on me and think they have a say in what goes on in my life with God and with him.

I'll admit I've tramped down every feeling and emotion for over a year now. I didn't allow any kind of fondness for him to cloud my judgment or make me miss him for even a second. I embraced my frustration and anger and made no room for him to get back in. I didn't reminisce about our life, things that have happened, happiness or sorrow, I just kept living and moving forward and doing what needed to be done.

I've said it over and over again, "I will never take him back."

Truth be told I'm not sure I ever will, but I am his friend, I do love him, we are connected and in tune to one another completely.

I haven't told him about my Midgets because it's going to break his heart, he's sitting in jail, there's nothing he can do about it and why hurt him that way? He talked to me that day and called me back the next morning because he said he knew something was wrong and wanted to make sure I was alright.

I don't trust him, believe anything he says and I hate what I feel like when he's here: having to know where the keys are, where my pocket book is, waking in the middle of the night to make sure he's still here. Its no way to live with someone, always worried they are going to go off the deep and end up back in the streets, dreading what they are going to take with them when that happens.

$6000 and a car is what it cost me this last time. Truth be told I'm not mad about the car because I bought it to protect the truck. No sense in both of us sitting in jail, right?

He can only receive post cards where he's at this time, so there will not be stacks of letters to keep when he gets out, although I'm working on a folder of required reading for him, for when he gets to the next place in his journey and truth be told I've actually set him up to fail.

He's got three years to do what he needs to do with God, a year in jail and two at Canaan Land and yes I know the program is only for a year, but that cat is getting two, don't care how it happens, just praying it happens.

If he's not sincere and just trying to talk game, he's going to fail.

That's three years God has to change my heart as well, because when I say I'm through, I'm through. I'm not going to live that way ever again. I'm not taking everything I have and handing it over ever again. He's gonna have to cough up some effort and some provision and he's going to have to grow up.

In order to even ask me on a date, he's going to have to pull off those three years.

Forgiveness Because You Can't Do It Enough

You don't know what they did to me Darlene.

They hurt me.

I know, I've been hurt too.

I'll never forgive them for what they did to me.

You're going to have to if you want to get better.

But you don't know what they did.

I don't have to know, the same kinds of things have happened to me too.

We have a tendency to hold tight to things: pain, hurts, baggage, every little thing that made us feel a certain kind of way.

Holding on to those kinds of things is like trying to hold a handful of sand, it's all slipping through your fingers in the first place, but still you hold tight. The tighter you try to grasp it the more it slips away.

Your pain can be a prison or a platform, it's always your choice.

What are you going to do with it?

If you make it your prison, it's going to make you sick and take you to some deep dark places. It's gonna twist you up and mess up your heart as well as your head.

When we hold on to those pains, we lay awake at night, thinking about what happened, letting it play over and over again in our heads like some bad re-run. We plot our revenge, what we'll say, how that person will react, but its all a lie. The scenario will never play out the way we imagine it and half the time those people have moved on and forgotten all about what they've done to us.

But you don't know what they did to me Darlene.

I'm not standing here telling you it doesn't matter because it does, but what matters more is you being healed and whole.

You matter more.

Yes you.

You matter so much more than the stuff you're caught up in right this second.

What matters more is the state of your heart and moving forward.

What matters more is breaking you out of that prison, so you can breathe again.

And stop listening to and talking to the chatter box!

Just stop!

It never says anything nice, not ever!

Forgiveness is a choice and you may have to do it more than once. You might even have to do it a bunch of times for a very long time until you really are over it.

You can start with forgiving yourself.

We've all done dumb stuff, gotten into situations because of bad choices, chosen the wrong people to love, the list goes on and on, but I want you to know it's okay to forgive yourself.

Life is happening to each and every one of us and we all play a part in that.

Forgive yourself. It's okay to do that.

Now, forgive them.

But you don't know Darlene.

I don't need to know.

Forgive them.

But they hurt me.

I know it was terrible, they were absolutely the worst for hurting you that way and I'm

sorry.

Forgive them.

Nothing anyone else does is because of you.

I know you find that hard to believe right this second but it's true.

Forgive them.

The chains are going to start breaking, your heart is going to eventually stop hurting,

your mind is going to stop keeping you awake at night with all those crazy plots it's got

going on and you will begin to live again.

You will pick up the pieces and hold your head high and begin the forward movement

your life requires.

I know it's hard, don't think I don't.

I'm having to do the same thing.

It takes practice and I've had lots of practice.

Forgive them.

Now breathe.

That's it, take a long deep breath and let it out.

Forgive them.

They can't hurt me anymore. I forgive them.

I'm not going to hold on to this any longer. I forgive them.

If you choose not to forgive them they will always have power over you.

How dumb is it to enslave yourself to someone who probably hasn't given you a second thought since the thing happened?

Forgive them.

I didn't say it was going to be easy, I even told you it could take a few times, but you can do it. I believe in you.

Don't you want to be free? To breathe? To be able to laugh and to smile again?

Forgive them.

If you don't believe I'm doing the same thing my husband left me a year ago, took the car, said all sorts of terrible things to me and this was after he'd taken everything we owned to the dope man. He left me with my truck in the shop, a baby and $6000 in debt for his stuff.

He didn't even say goodbye. We were in the bed taking a nap when it happened.

I never got the car back, I'm still paying for it.

Sixteen years this has been going on, him actively addicted carrying everything off, while I'm clean and busting my tail to pay for all of it.

I forgive him.

But how can you do that Darlene?

I have to for me.

I have to because Jesus forgave me.

I have to because I can't use any of it to move forward into my destiny.

I have to because of grace.

I forgive him, like I've forgiven him so many times before.

I told you I've had a lot of practice.

I'm not by any means excusing his behavior or letting him off the hook for treating me second best. I can't do anything about any of that, but in order for my heart to be right, to be healed and whole I forgive him.

What kind of person do I look like loving everyone but him?

I forgive him.

Jesus forgave me everything. He forgave me being an addict and a prostitute. He welcomed me with open arms.

He's never thrown it in my face or reminded me of any of it.

I've been forgiven so much, I can forgive this one thing.

I'm taking that pain and using it as a platform in hopes it will help you or someone else.

Forgiveness is healing me every moment of every day.

Don't you want to be healed too?

Forgive them.

I love you so much thanks for letting me share.

Update: this entire piece ended up being about me and I'm not forgiving anyone. I'm just fine with that. People deserted me, turned on me, shunned me and some of them tried shaming me.

I look back over all these old posts and it's no wonder my mental illness was alive and well, I was bat shit crazy!

When you open your eyes and change your mind about things, you are amazed at the bullshit you allowed yourself to believe.

My eyes are wide open and people are free to whatever they like, I'd just prefer they not share it with me.

I was very angry at first, all messed up. I didn't know what I would do with my life. There was no one to lay in bed and talk to at night, because no one was ever there listening in the first place.

It's totally a thing of the past for me today.

The Dream

It's bubbling and growing and getting bigger with every day.

It's a dream of stadium sized proportions and it's only just begun.

I have to do something! I just can't sit idly by, it's not in my dna.

I'm about to get non profit status which opens up doors and avenues and all sorts of things that aren't possible without it.

God has been talking to my heart about my people in the streets for a very long time, showing me how there could be a different kind of shelter, a home for those without one.

As we're growing up and having dreams about what we want our lives to look like, I don't think there is a soul alive that says or thinks I'm gonna love homeless people when I grow up.

I'm still in awe of what God has called me do.

It wasn't that moment when I said to Him, "What do you want me to do." It wasn't something I purposed to do and even though I'd been in the streets and continued to go back to them and serve, He pretty much dragged me kicking and screaming into the it all. I wanted stadiums, He kept saying "the streets are bigger." I wanted to evangelize the world and He kept saying, "you're needed in the streets."

Funniest part of all is I've never given the first sermon.

You know it's love when it's at least ninety degrees outside and you're still hugging and loving on sweaty stinky homeless people.

I'm believing God for a homeless shelter, for recovery houses, for a pool hall, laundromats, self sustaining ministry. I'm believing God to do what God does, the impossible.

I'm believing He can do anything and this is a purpose He has for my life.

Update: Never happened.

People don't want to support homeless people. People don't want to support people who want to support homeless people.

It's not my dream any longer. That chapter has closed and today I am worrying about me, about saving me, about making my own life better.

Religion makes you feel like you're not worth a shit and how dare you want other things than what we tell you to want.

It marks you with guilt and calls you selfish. It steals your identity so you can be some clone, another sheep.

We Do Not Protest The Protesters

Yesterday something totally new and different happened to me and it was astonishing as well as amazing.

We went to the pride march and stood on the steps of the capital with signs of love and support for those in that community.

There were protesters there and I've decided for the entirety of my lifetime I will never protest the protesters.

What can you say to them to change their minds? Nothing.

They believe they are right and it's just the way it is.

It's alright. I don't have to respond. I refuse to make myself look crazy to those who don't know me trying to prove a point. Not my style. In this case I believe my silence speaks much louder than words.

I have no desire to shout louder than them whatsoever.

It was totally cool and made me feel so powerful walking away with a smile on their face asking our Daddy to fix their hearts.

All I could keep thinking to myself was "All that love going to waste over something they've wrongly been taught."

I'm choosing happiness, peace, silence, to smile and to pray.

I am a force to be reckoned with even in my silence.

My silence shows more strength than anything I've ever said in my life.

I am changing, I am becoming, I am creating and I am not in debt to any man, not even for a response.

I am changing the way I see the world, the things that come out of my mouth, the things I allow my brain to believe and I have no lack whatsoever in my life.

I need nothing.

I am whole.

I have everything.

I am everything.

I am the kingdom of God and I do not have to respond to those set on insulting and railing and condemning. God does not need me to defend Him.

He needs me to keep looking like His son, Jesus.

Did I tell you how cool I know I look, wearing those sandals and those fine clothes? He may have been homeless but they gambled for His clothes. The man could dress people. Think about it.

You look like Jesus, meaning you have long hair, fine clothes, sandals on your feet and a beard. :)

I look so cool strolling off.

Nothing to worry about.

Smiling and just easing on down the road.

Nothing wrong with that image of yourself. He's madly in love you with you. He thinks you are so amazing. He wants you to have it all.

People don't erect statues for critics.

Walk away, talk to Big Daddy, keep your peace and your dignity. Love wins.

Can you imagine the train wreck of love that becomes when those hearts discover how wrong they've been and God shows them the people He loves they hurt with their wrong belief?

Boom!

Come Lord Jesus, come!

Spoiler alert. We're all gonna make it!

Nothing can separate us from His love!

Update: God doesn't show them anything, they are mean and hateful and they keep going day after day washed in their ignorance and spreading it around on everyone else. I absolutely despise the ones who show up just to argue and prove how stupid they really are. They know it all, there's nothing you could know more than them. You're going to find out one day. Just wait until you're dead. You're going to meet him. I could go on for days with the lame ass shit they say and that's what it is "shit".

The Big Lie Brought Me To The Truth And Gave Me Something Worth Living For

They say "You ain't leavin unless it's in a body bag".

Look here partner, I came in a body bag, I'm still wearing that thing and making it look good!

I'm about to explode with excitement!

When I think about where I came from and how far God has brought me to today!

Mercy!

He had a plan for me!

He wanted me to live and not die!

He brought me up out of that place, hell if you will, because it sure wasn't heaven there.

Its been stirring in me all day!

He had a plan for my life!

Amen somebody!

I didn't even know I was going to meet Him, I just knew I had to go.

I saw a couple of pastor's posts today where they posted the place where their lives changed forever, where they finally met God and understood what it all meant.

He brought me out the streets.

He gave me a new name!

He gave me a purpose I never would've seen coming!

He gave me dreams bigger than anyone will ever believe come true, but you best believe those bad boys are going to come true and greater things than these will I do.

My Daddy owns everything and it's His good pleasure to do for me, so you just stay tuned and see what the Lord has done.

I'm going places! I'm building a legacy! I'm attracting great wealth and influence every moment of every day and there's gonna come a day when I get to walk in the fullness of my calling.

I'm planning book signings, painting exhibits, groups, teams, churches, conferences, businesses and things so grand I cry every time I think about them.

My grandchildren are going to walk into ministry because Nanny did it. My children are going to prosper and shake their heads at the things they see their mother do.

My husband is going to stand back in amazement knowing it was true when I said it! The bible says a man's gift will make room for him and bring him into the presence of kings and great men.

I tell my daughter in law all the time, you know me, but wait until you see what God is about to let me do.

Wait until you see all these dreams you've been hearing me talk about come true.

I'm going to sell out conferences because people are hurting and need someone to come along and remind them who they are and in those cities we're going to go into the streets and search for people to feed while we're there.

I saw a movie this past week with my girlfriends and the entire time I sat in that theater I cried and saw me on that movie screen, I saw my life unfolding for others to see, I saw my dreams coming into existence. It wasn't even a sad movie y'all! God kept saying to me, "that's you girl, you can do that, I know you want it, I'm going to give it to you." I couldn't even talk when I left, tears still streaming down my cheeks.

I want to further the kingdom!

Somebody better tell that other woman preacher my name because she and I need to get together and talk about some things!

Lover's Lane has only just begun and I'm already restless for so much more.

I am that girl!

I am God's willing vessel!

I am a voice for the kingdom! I am completely sold out for Jesus and I don't care what you tell me I'm gonna change the world!

That girl that came out the streets, broken, strung out, used up and without hope is no more.

He brought out of the valley of the shadow of death and I didn't even have the good sense to be scared while I was down there.

I'm not satisfied!

I want more!

To do more, see more, be more and say more!

All for Jesus!

All for his people!

All for the kingdom!

When Father? When?

I'm realistic I believe for miracles every single day! I want it all! I get excited and worked up over every single little thing I get to do and you know what? Until now, it has never turned out the way I thought it would and even now is questionable and I totally hate this feeling of discouragement and not knowing and wondering why oh why do I do this?

I have to be real about this!

They called me about the Sparky Babies Car Show yesterday, for the second time in a year asking if we were on. No we aren't, but please call me again next year, because I'd love to do another.

There's no food for the streets again.

Walked into today believing for two thousand dollars plus and walked away with $25 feeling like I should have given one of the paintings away to a boy.

When is it really going to be my turn Daddy?

When do I get to be the one with all the toys, because I have so many I want to give them away to?

Update: He never answered me, he never sent me any kind of sign, he simply faded into the background along with the people who claimed to love him. I can't tell you how broken hearted I was being alone, deconstructing, trying to figure out what to do next with my life.

Who Cares?

Lately I'm at a place of such great peace I keep hearing "who cares?" over and over again in my head.

I care but not in the ways others do.

I'm a different season of my life today, peaceful and prospering.

It's exhausting trying to straighten everyone out so I choose not to do it.

If people want to wrongly believe things, let them! God has been letting it go on from the beginning. He's not worried about it, He never was.

Social media can be a blessing or a curse, I choose the blessing. I'm growing my influence, putting out a good message, sharing love with everyone and I don't want to be involved in anything else.

I'm stepping back from certain situation including church to figure out some things.

I want more, actually I want it all and there's no one in the world who can tell me I can't have it.

I want great influence so I can help to change the lives of millions.

I want overflowing abundance in my life and plenty of money to support my answer to prayer endeavors.

I want to do conferences every weekend, absolutely everywhere!

I want to do outreach in each of those cities.

I want to be surrounded by people who celebrate me.

I'm not saying there aren't people in my life who celebrate me, I'm just saying there are not enough people in my life who celebrate me because I spend a lot of time lately feeling like I'm standing on the outside looking in.

Ministry requires revenue and that energy just isn't arriving from the places I think it should, so I'm looking for the unexpected places, for the places no one else thought to look.

I am in great expectancy of the things to come, for every dream I have to come true and for life to continue to move me into my destiny at any moment now. It's on the way, I'm ready for it, I am excited about it and unfortunately everyone is not called to go on that trip with me.

I want more from my life than the people who told me they loved me just because they saw me at church.

I want to do more, to be more, to experience more and be the answer to more people's prayers.

I want to inspire others to do the same.

This past weekend was so exciting, so much so that when I went back to work on Monday, I kind of felt deflated about the entire situation. I love my job, I just have to find the enjoyment in it again.

I am meant for so much more and I want it.

God has brought me a mighty long way and there is so such a long way to go.

I've been incubating, learning, believing, studying new things and I am not satisfied to stay where I am.

I have a new direction to go in for absolutely everything in my life.

When I see the stuff that goes on, people speaking from a place of fear because they've believed a religious lie "Who cares?" comes around and I keep moving. I can't fix anybody, most people will refuse to change their minds even on their deathbeds, so why spend so much time trying to fix it? I'm not doing that anymore. I have a higher calling than that, more important things to do.

I won't apologize for any of it.

There's so much to experience in the world, beauty, love, life and laughter, getting all twisted up in what other people believe is total nonsense.

Saw a post yesterday about a statue that's on display somewhere and the woman who posted it was so frightened, something that has absolutely no power and she's totally freaking out. No time for that, love heals the nations. It wouldn't have mattered what I said to her about it, she'd already made up her mind to be afraid and to believe there was something in it.

I know it's total nonsense, others know the same, but she's convinced about it, so why waste time trying to correct her wrong thinking?

There's so much that's wrong in the world, but that's not nor will it ever be my focus. I want to focus on what's right with it, what's good and beautiful. I want to stay focused on Jesus and all the wonderful plans He has for me.

Who cares?

I care but not in the way you want me to.

I'm looking for the good in everything and I know it's there.

I'm looking for the beautiful in every situation because I know it can be found.

I'm not doing this back and forth thing anymore.

I've got my vision, I'm ready to go, everyone is welcome to come with me and those who don't just won't be seeing very much of me anymore, because it takes participation to see dreams come true, it requires effort to move into destiny.

Update: No one ever shows up and or wants to go. People are lazy, they want you to do it until it's big then they want to jump on board for you. Over the years I did manifest the life I'm living now, through talking about other dreams. I did that, no god assisted me.

I'm living my best life ever, without any of the nonsense I used to believe and even though I'm still very mentally ill at times, I love my life and I've never been happier. Church folks do what makes them feel good until they have to put effort and sacrifice into it. People came with me three times in all those years of going. Their favorite thing to do was tell me they'd like to go some times.

For the first time in my life I get to concentrate on me, on what I want, where I'm going, without any outside influences and or insanity. I'm free, living alone, being an adult and it's so much better than all of this. I can't say enough how much better it is.

I Was An Addict Who Chose To Love An Addict And Here We Are Today

Has your heart ever been so raw that everything hurts? No matter what it is you feel

assaulted and beat down and wronged.

The slightest situation makes you feel as though the world is caving in and going to end.

Man! It's tough!

It's only a moment in time and it's usually a lie.

I have a beautiful life.

I have my peace, I have great joy, I sleep well at night and even though I experience

mental illness and depression from time to time, I am well.

I made a decision to love someone, knowing that someone was messed up, had never

had a normal life and nothing to offer me.

That's what love does. It believes the best of everyone, it's not looking for anything for

itself and it has this uncontrollable hope that springs up and believes miracles can

happen, no matter what.

I've spent seventeen years with and without the same man.

He's done me dirty, stolen from me, made me feel less then, left me alone and left me.

Underneath my anger and frustration and disappointment that love is still there, because

that's the choice I made.

He's an addict, he's always been an addict and I'd like to think he's not always going to

be an addict, but I can't see the future, I can only go on what I have already experienced.

When you love someone like that, you go through the things you go through with them, go through things alone without them and have a life to live outside of their drama you learn to turn your heart on and off like a water faucet.

You have to or you'll die from the disappointment and hurt.

You have to to make it to work every day, to pay your bills, to love your kids, your grand kids, those around you. You have to learn to live outside the parameters of the addiction and what that does to your life.

You try to second guess them, to protect them, to help them and you try to protect yourself.

There's no protection in love, it's all in, or it's not love.

Seventeen years.

For seventeen years I've tried to help him, to get him help, to be the best wife I could possibly be, to be a best friend and to be the example.

I was homeless, strung out and jumping in and out of cars when I met him and made that decision to love him. I loved him before I ever even knew his name, the moment I laid eyes on him. I loved him.

I knew what he was, I knew what I was, there were no disillusions in that decision.

We fought like cats and dogs, I hid, he searched, it's a wonder still, all these years later.

It's truly sad, some of it, seventeen years. I can only remember a couple of Thanksgivings, two or three Christmas's, a couple of birthdays. When you break down 17 years, him serving time for over ten of them, getting high three fourths of the rest of the time, you're left with a small amount of happiness and memories.

My fondest memory is a recent one, probably three or four years ago, dancing in the living room to Al Green one Saturday night.

An addict can't take you out to eat, can't pay for your movie tickets, can't help pay bills or buy groceries. An addict can't keep their promises.

I stopped taking his calls from the jail back in November because I can't and won't go back. I can't live that way anymore. You jump out of bed to make sure they are still there, you have to know where the keys are, you have to know where the money is, you wonder if you hid those things well enough, you have to be in control which makes you out of control. When they leave the house to go to the convenience store you wonder if they will come back and there's this huge rock in the bottom of your stomach all the time. You don't trust anything they say or do because they've never given you any reason to, but still that hope springs eternal.

He got out yesterday morning and I got the dreaded phone call, the one I didn't want.

I yelled, I cussed, I cried and for the first time ever, probably, I was completely honest with him about how I feel about him, what I'm willing to do and not do, what he would have to do to get back in my good graces and how I am so sick of his shit.

The last thing he said to me was, "I'm willing to do anything I have to to have my wife and my family back."

He was in the streets getting high before dark.

You have your resolve and then they come along carrying all that love you've had for them and you get all twisted up with hope again, wanting to help, wanting to believe, wanting something better for them.

You think about all the people you love in the streets and how their lives look so similar and everyone needs to be loved, because love wins.

You think about who you are and how you should treat this person, because they are sick and need help.

You think about how people are going to think you're stupid the minute they hear the first piece of news about him, or her.

You think about how others will judge you because you've done this so many times before.

All the terrible stuff you've already been through goes through your mind and your heart suddenly feels sick and heavy.

No matter how loudly your brain is screaming your heart has that flame of hope that springs eternal and you want to do whatever is best for them in the situation, because love covers a multitude of sins. Love keeps giving and forgiving and giving again.

In those moments it doesn't matter what they've done, how wronged you've been, how deep your disappointment and betrayal is, you just want to help.

Let's keep it real this is someone you love, this is not some entity out to get you and suck you back into the life you used to have.

One thing I've known since the day I left the streets was if I wanted to go and get high, I was going to get high and the choice was always mine. I've had plenty of money to do it, been in all the right places to get it, still go to the streets today. The choice has never

crossed my mind, even if the thought were there. I chose.

I was sick and tired of being sick and tired and I chose to love him.

I've spent the money to divorce him twice and I'm still his wife.

When my court date came up last time, I just couldn't hurt him that way, no matter what

he'd done to me. I just didn't have the heart to do it.

Is he a nice guy? I really don't know anymore. I know he's never been mean to me, he's

never put his hands on me and when he's good he's really good. He's likable, friendly,

and outgoing just like me.

Underneath all that junk is the person he really is.

I've had glimpses of that person over the years and that person is who has kept me

loving him, looking for the good in him, believing for his miracle.

The heart wants what the heart wants and man oh man the things the heart wants.

Underneath all that garbage and drama and bullshit is a man I chose to love seventeen

years ago.

I've chosen not to take the same roads I've traveled with him and I've had to shut him out

of my life, but that does not stop my heart from being my heart.

I don't want to be his wife anymore but I don't want to hurt him either.

I know that sounds crazy, but I don't hold grudges and I used to be him, miserable,

strung out, longing for more and only a fool would believe he isn't unhappy and longing

for more.

I sit here tonight knowing he must be miserable, knowing he blew it and only that. I can't read his mind, I don't know any more than that, but I know if I the situation was reversed I would be very unhappy and trying to figure out how to fix it even though I messed it up.

I'm saying all of this because the most beautiful thing about life is we are never alone and we are not the only one. Someone needs to hear this because their own heart is hurting and they are in a catch twenty two with someone just like him. There's a mother who is almost ninety years old in Atlanta Georgia tonight whose heart is broken yet again, a heart that has been broken many more times than my own. There are others all over just like us, who don't understand, who have been wronged, disappointed, and ripped off by someone they love who is strung out on drugs.

Someone has to talk about it!

Someone has to say something for everyone.

Someone has to tell their story so someone else can survive.

I don't struggle with it, but I know there are many that do.

I'm on both sides of the fence, I've been there and now I'm somewhere else.

I want someone, anyone who needs it to be encouraged because this is not the end, even though it may feel like it some times.

I want someone who is struggling to get some courage to keep facing today, because no one is promised tomorrow and it's a journey that's difficult even under the best of circumstances.

We get so caught up in the happening of it all, we lose sight of the people who are trapped in their own choices, messed up, messing up, destroying their lives and the lives of those they love because they need drugs to cope with some underlying issue they just can't face yet.

I want you to know there is life after drugs and it can be so abundant, filled with joy and peace. I want you to know you are not the only one and the more you face it and talk about it and make others aware of it, the more people you have in your corner fighting for you, cheering you on. I want you to know that no matter what you deserve to have a great life, to be well and have peace in your heart.

What you've done is not what's important, what you're doing now is.

I'm living proof you can make it.

I'm living proof its not going to kill you.

I'm living proof that love really does win.

I want you to know that even if you mess up, it's not the end and you can make the choice to start over, minute by minute. Life is starting over and over again.

It doesn't matter if those you've hurt have forgiven you because God's forgiveness has always been there, over and over and over again and will always be there, over and over and over again. He doesn't hold grudges just like me, stop holding grudges with yourself!

Give yourself a break, you've made a long and painful journey to get to today.

You are valuable, you are loved, you are more than enough!

Keep trying, keep getting back up and brushing yourself off, you're going to make it!

If no one else believes in you I do!

I have to protect myself, so he can't come back, but I still want to help him and given the opportunity I will, for now I have to turn off that water faucet and keep moving like I always do, whether it feels fair to me or not.

I'm okay with that.

I'm sending you lots of love.

I'm sending you courage.

Don't give up.

Update: Walking away is always a good thing to do in these situations.

I don't feel like I wasted any of that time, there was a great lesson to learn in all of it.

I'm loving my divorce and wouldn't take it back on a bet.

I meant what I said when I said I'd never speak to him again and he's never heard from me since the day I kicked him out.

I'm not pining away for someone to love.

I don't feel incomplete or broken.

I'm having the time of my life.

Have a friend who is getting divorced, their entire drama has played out on social media and all she can talk about is finding someone else to love. If you don't love yourself and find out who you are you are in no position to love anyone else.

I don't need it. I don't want it. I'm happy to be on my own. I don't need anyone.

Love is grand but it's also a huge pain in the ass, it's painful, it can hurt you more than anything on the face of the planet.

I'm not looking for love, I don't need it, I have plenty of it. My children and grandchildren love me. My dog loves me more than any human on the face of the planet.

I'm wore out on relationships. I don't have the patience for it right now. I have no interest in being sexual with anyone and that's the only reason a man chases a woman to begin with.

I had a friend I sort of liked but when I told him he never spoke to me again.

I don't have room for anyone, literally. I bought a camper for the dog and me and that's all the room there is in it. It's Sparky sized. I'm so in love with it, it's the first new thing I've ever been able to buy and it's mine, my home, everything I need to live where I am. I lived in it for nearly three weeks without electricity, just a drop chord from my girl's house.

I had to get it moved before the weather got warmer, for the dog. It's heaven on earth, the only heaven I've ever known in my entire life.

I Love You So Much

I love that moment in time when you realize it's just you, He's right there with you, it's okay, everything is going to be alright.

Last night I put on some blues. Yes, I like me some slow feeling sorry for myself blues.

I unplug FINALLY!

IT'S SO HARD!

Start pouring out paint, the backgrounds have been done, create something.

This morning I've got a 639 Hz , get this LOL. Attract love, raise positive energy, Marimba Meditation Music. I'm painting, I'm being, I'm creating and I am with God.

Exhale.

Inhale.

Hold it.

Exhale.

It's okay!

It's going to be okay!

You are going to be okay!

I'm going to be okay!

It's not going to kill you I promise!

Breathe!

Give yourself a break!

It's not that serious.

Give yourself a chance to relax, once second. Just suddenly remember to smile.

See!

Don't you feel better?

You did it, I know you did!

It's great!

You're beautiful, you're awesome and you're gonna have a great day!

I love you so much!

I'm going to be a painter now, bye.

I began studying energy and the law of manifestation, it was a welcome distraction and I can't even begin to tell you all the things I've manifested.

There is absolutely no truth in religion.

I Know What I Know Because I Know It's My Truth And I Know That I Know That I Know

Rays of sunshine.

Look, I get it, but are you going to choose to be positive or be negative?

If you get up cursing the day the moment your feet hit the floor then what kind of day do you think you are going to have? "I don't want to get up this morning." Well, why not? It's a whole day of possibilities stretched out in front of you. You tell the day you don't want to get up, you're telling the day you don't want to participate. So, the day says to itself, "Okay, I won't let you have a good day then, if that's the way you're going to be about it."

Are you going to see your life as constantly falling apart and struggling or are you going to count the good stuff, focus on the better stuff, be thankful for the little stuff and keep right on moving in a positive vibration into the unknown stuff.

I don't want to be unhappy or sad. EVER!

I want every day to bring me something new and something beautiful and the love of my creator.

Those moments when He comes close to me, when I'm overwhelmed with love and understanding and freely flowing tears.

You can seek answers your entire life, every moment of every day, but that one moment, is without description, needs no answers, translations, it needs nothing. A huge breath, love overflowing, tears, laughter, ah ha moments. That's all that matters in all of space, time, eternity, kingdom and understanding, that one moment when you know God is there, He's loving you, He's smiling at you, He's always welcoming you into His arms. You can show me things in the text, you can show me truths, you can point me in the direction to find answers, but you cannot under any circumstances tell me there isn't a God.

I've felt Him, I'm not crazy, I don't do drugs anymore, I know He was there. Whoever He is, Whatever He is, All that He is, Everything He is and all that love everyone is always talking about. If everyone is talking about how good it is, then you already know how good it is. Taste and see that the Lord is good.

I believe all sorts of different things today and in case no one has noticed I'm not chatting too much about it, but it does not change my love for God. It doesn't change the love other people have for their God. It doesn't change the love affair I'm having with my creator, whether I can prove He exists or not, no matter what text says, what scrolls say, what books, critics and other believers say. What I believe is no one's business but my own, it is between me and my creator.

Who cares what I believe?

I believe I will love people.

I believe I will love myself.

I believe love wins.

I believe love heals the nations.

I believe it doesn't matter what I believe.

I believe I'll stay in this positive vibration, oneness, perfect union, in the greatest love affair of all time with the creator of the universe! If I'm wrong it's still so amazing and who are you to take it from me?

What if everybody is wrong?

Love, love, love, all ya need is love!

Update: We follow along without ever questioning anything because that's how its presented to you. Furthermore so me preachers will go off the grid if you ask questions. It's the biggest sham in the world.

I hate to be lied to and that's exactly what all of it is, a well executed lie that people have gone along with for so long they believe it's true.

How did I get that far off into the deep end without asking questions? What the hell could I have been thinking?

I almost hate that girl I used to be, so ignorant and uneducated about what I thought I believed. It didn't take long for the whole house of cards to come tumbling down once I started asking questions.

That One Call That Changes Everything

Man oh man this love thing is something serious!

A picture is worth a thousand words right? This picture has reeled me in time and time again.

Anyone who knows me knows the story of Antoine and me. We've been together and apart for seventeen years. We met in the streets, both of us addicted to crack. Seventeen years of prison sentences, jail time, street time and then there's the precious good times, few and far between. We've had a couple of Thanksgiving's together, a couple of birthdays together and two or three Christmas's. We've had one anniversary together that I can remember. Seventeen years.

He's been struggling that entire time, doing stupid stuff, hurting me, hurting himself and his mother.

I've only seen him once since he left almost two years ago and that time was frightening and sad.

I've taken calls and I've not taken calls. I've been nice and I've been mean. I've been hurt and I've been disappointed to the point you just have to turn it all off and keep going.

People can say whatever they like about all of it, I really don't care. No one has ever had to hear me cry about it. I've shed all my tears in silence and the privacy of my bedroom. People will say they will do anything for love, but will they really?

I've been embarrassed and felt like everyone thought I was a fool but that doesn't matter because love covers a multitude of sins. Love forgives and gives again and again, without holding grudges and without fear.

I chose him in the midst of hell.

I chose to love him no matter the odds.

I chose to take the wild ride without knowing how wild it was going to be.

I've paid my price and then some and then some more.

No matter what I say or do he keeps coming back with "I love you,", "It's okay, it's not your fault,", "Please don't give up on me," and "I want to come home."

No matter how long I don't take his calls he keeps calling until I finally do and he's never mad or fussing at me about it.

The world only sees what's wrong with him, the wrong he's done, the things he doesn't seem to be willing to fix, but I see him. I see that gorgeous black boy standing at the end of the street the night we met, tall and proud. I see the man who cried his eyes out watching The Notebook. I see the man who writes me love letters, who sings to me, tries making me laugh and who dances with me where ever and when ever I ask. I see the man who busts out singing Al Green in the Waffle House. I see the man my heart has set itself upon, for better or worse.

I wish I could say it's been beautiful.

I wish I could tell you things have been just fine.

I wish I could give you this long drawn out happy story about what our marriage has been like, but I can't.

Seventeen years is a long time.

He's put me through hell, made me mad, disappointed me, hurt me and gave me great joy.

I love him.

I can't do anything about it and believe me I've tried.

I've only asked for one thing in all those years, step away from life, go somewhere and find God.

I've prayed, I've cried, I've waited, I've suffered, I've believed, I've started over again and again. I've paid off all the stuff, the fines, the dope men. I've written letters for years and spent years alone.

I've walked around feeling half complete, I've walked around feeling whole.

I don't need him, I love him.

Wednesday at 2:30 my life and his life change forever.

He's finally made the call and is going.

It's his only choice.

Go to Canaan Land for two years or we have nothing to talk about.

Love has boundaries I've discovered and mine are drawn now, I can't and won't go back.

We have to go forward from here, try the one thing that hasn't been tried and believe for the best.

He's finally sick and tired of being sick and tired.

He's finally giving me the one thing I've wanted.

It changes everything, absolutely everything!

I've promised to support him 100% if he goes.

That means for the next two years I'm going to church somewhere else, I'm showing up for all those visits, for whatever is needed of me. I don't know what it all looks like but I know one thing for sure I will support him.

I'd also like to think if the roles were reversed he would do the same for me.

I'll find out whose really riding with us during that time, who my real friends are, who really truly does love us and wants to see us succeed.

I can't be afraid, it's a lie.

When I go to pick him up it'll be the first time in almost two years my husband will have held me, will have kissed me, will have pleasantly been in my presence.

I'm turning him over to God.

We'll deconstruct later, LOL.

Pray for us.

Update: If anyone actually did pray for us, it didn't work and or their god didn't hear them or honor their prayers.

It was terrible! He was an inconsiderate asshole the entire time he was here. He was noisy and selfish and had a bad attitude.

I was so stressed out I drank constantly, day and night. I just recently finished a health journey and lost fifty pounds, after getting so big I couldn't get my shoes on.

He made sure to tell me what a fat bitch I was before leaving and in nasty voice mails.

Those middle of the night calls ended when I changed my phone number.

It was never "I miss you,", or "I love you," calls it was always some crazy shit, threats, saying fowl things to me.

Peace is priceless and I now see how my peace kept getting destroyed over and over again, because I was insane. I was doing the same thing over and over again expecting different results.

He didn't really want to be married, he just wanted somewhere to land until he got to feeling good again.

He left with clothes I bought him that still had tags on them. He had a truck load of stuff and I was glad to let him have it. I threw everything else out.

If he's not happy and didn't get what he wanted, oh well, it was his choice.

After he left he got another phone, probably for a week hahahaha, started sending me pictures of crack he was smoking, blocked that account and went on with my life. I even deleted his facebook, because I'm the one that made it and it was always mine for game.

The Bible

As I move into the next part of this story there are many things that have changed, drastic changes. Some of it you would find hard to believe.

This walk I was on began in 2004 when I met Randy Bohrer and JT.

They bought me a McArthur New King James Study Bible and sent me to Set Free.

I had a 13+ years love affair with that bible. I read it at work, I read it waiting in line, I read it on the trains and the buses, I read it laying in bed at night. I never stopped reading it for all those years.

When I'd finally read the cover off it, I took neon orange duct tape and taped it back together, because there was no way I was letting someone have it six or more weeks to rebind it. Nope, not happening. That's my sword! Gotta have it.

It still has that duct tape on it today, only now it's also in a pink and orange paisley bible cover that has a cross on the front of it. It zips up, but probably never has been.

I worked in a gas station from 2009 to 2013 and my bible sat there on the counter all day, every day.

When the manager was mean to me, I read my bible. When I was lonely for my husband, I read my bible. When I was happy and life was going just fine, I read my bible.

People started bringing me books.

When I moved back to Atlanta in 2013, to be with my husband, I carried a uhaul full of books home to Atlanta. I used to read all the time. I could read a full length novel inside of two days, at work.

I can read the bible cover to cover in thirty days, being lazy and reading the new testament over and over again during that time. I was at Set Free for not quite 60 days and I read it three times cover to cover before I left there.

I came back to Alabama not two months later, the husband carried off all the books and sold my grand daddy's stereo to some crack dealer, before I could get back to retrieve them. The rest were burned up in a fire. I packed sixteen boxes of books into that uhaul.

I have 4 bibles, at present. My tried and true, A 400th Anniversary edition King James Study bible, a large print I ran across cleaning out a unit and a small black one I call my preacher bible. I don't like the ones that have "holy bible" written on them and not one of mine do.

You would be surprised how many people don't read it. You've be even more surprised at the ones who haven't read it all.

I guess-timate I've read the bible cover to cover over a 100 times. The math says if I read it once every thirty days for that amount of time it would be 153. The New Testament got 300 or more reads, easy. I would read it over and over again, write sermons, make notes.

I've had people try to insult me by saying I've read it that much but couldn't possibly understand what it is saying. I've heard all sorts of silly things.

I've had a guy in a group I assumed was full of halfass scholars tell me he hasn't read the entire thing yet.

How are you going to debate and argue and proof a book you haven't even read?

That's like Cliff Notes for a chemistry test.

People don't read it, they just go around beating the hell out of everyone else with it and the god they claim is love.

At first I was amazed, now it's my number one question and I am never surprised by the answer and or not getting one. Most of the time people refuse to answer and that tells me all I need to know. I'm never nasty about it, because I really don't care, but it's interesting to see how quickly they become offended or have nothing else to say. One simple question. How many times would you say you've read the bible cover to cover?

Trust and believe I have read the bible. I have read the bible a lot. I have living eye witnesses to my claim of reading the bible and three sons who were there the entire time.

I had a relationship with the bible like no other relationship I've ever had in my life.

I wanted to know. I had to have the answers. I had to find what everyone else claimed was in there. I wanted to know that God so badly.

How many of you know if you stay with something long enough, you'll find some things out?

The Honeymoon Is Over

I spent most of my life, walking away, running away, letting things go and moving on. No stability whatsoever. My mother died right before I turned 21 and she was the only glue that held it all together.

She was good as gold and I was a selfish spoiled brat, her oldest daughter, strong and willful. She raised me to be that way, wanted me to be stronger than she had been and this caused great rifts in our relationship from time to time.

She gave me things I didn't care about, things I didn't know how to appreciate and she introduced me to chinese food. The chinese food is all I have left and it has been one of the greatest loves of my life.

She was a haridresser and though I didn't know it at the time, made me totally cool with all the stuff she did to my hair.

I'm 51 and I still miss her. She would have absolutely loved all of these children or our's, the grandchildren that have come along.

From the day she died I was pretty much homeless and remained that way until seventeen years ago.

The stability is really an illusion, things could change at any given moment.

I brought my husband home a few weeks ago, I am his home, I am where he belongs and no matter what has happened in the past, we have come to a new day and new decisions.

I knew there would be those who would turn their backs on me, those who would prove just how true their friendships are and those who just wouldn't care one way or another. People usually only love you when you're doing good, or when you're doing something that makes them happy. Rather than support you they want you to do what they think is the right thing and they don't usually take your heart into account when these things happen.

I knew this going in. I knew it was my decision and my life and my heart that were at stake and I knew the dangers involved when I drove to Atlanta to get him.

We've been through a lot and I said I would never let him come back but I'm full of it because my heart loves him so much no amount of time that passes between us, whether we are together or not, my heart belongs to him and continues to love him fiercely.

I knew things would change and they had been for some time to come before then. I've been studying and deconstructing and everything I believe has changed, including what I believe about others and it's my truths, no one else's.

I've been stepping away, questioning absolutely everything, watching what really goes on and making some decisions about my future, the one where my husband is in my life and the lives of my children and grandchildren.

Life reveals all its ugly secrets to you one at a time, glimpses of what you thought was real that wasn't and it comes in seasons and cycles as it has been designed to do. One at a time because your heart would break and kill you if you saw it all at once.

Most people don't know how or want to deal with their problems. They are famous for sweeping them under the rug like they don't matter. I have to face my problems head

on, its just the way I'm built. I've never had the luxury of having that broom or rug.
I already knew some things and had prepared my heart for those things in advance. I
knew people were going to reject me, reject him, I knew lines of allegiance would be
drawn and every fake thing in my life would be exposed.

These things were being revealed to me the entire time he was gone but I had to brace
and prepare myself for the rest.

The world is full of contradictions, like we're in this thing together but I don't owe you
anything. That's a good one. If you don't owe me anything then there is no way we
could be in this together, because you've already stated you have no obligations to me,
never mind love.

I love people hard, I commit hard, everything I do has a hardness and fierceness to it.
People do what makes them feel good as long as it makes them feel good, when they
have to sacrifice something of themselves or their time they usually won't do it for long.
The streets for instance, three people wanted to go and go all the time, another girlfriend
would have went all the time but her husband wasn't having it and even my children
only went out of obligation. Some went once just to see what it was like and the rest just
said how they were planning to go with me some time. After a while they even stopped
giving to it. Its okay, I have no problem with it, I still love them, I'm still gonna do what
I do and no amount of participation or lack thereof is going to change the course that's
been set before me.

There are huge things still in store for me, things I haven't gotten to yet.

I'm not settling for the ordinary, I am a beast.

My heart has been broken again and again by people I love, it happens all the time and it happens pretty frequently.

Rather than being bitter, I am choosing to walk away and to find new people. Yeah I know, I'm a glutton for punishment.

I'm not interested in excuses or prayers, I want action.

I have a handful of friends and even those change from time to time.

I get it, people have their own lives and that's just fine, I have one too, it's very busy and full and no one else can live it for me.

I am not too busy for those who are in need. I remember where I came from and there are those who still need to be brought out.

Some people make changes but the changes aren't real, they just aren't doing dope anymore.

Everything changed when he got back here, everything is going to keep changing and whatever I can't use that stuff has to go.

I was told "he needs to come to church.", no bro, you need to be the church.

I've drug that man to church after church, service after service for the entire time we've been together, I'm not pressuring him any longer. I'm giving him his freedom. If he wants to lay in the bed every Sunday while I go to church, that's just fine with me, because I am so happy and thankful he's in my bed sleeping. The church should be effective without people having to come for services.

We ran into some of "my people" and those people didn't even speak to him. You can be polite to someone you don't even like. He said it didn't bother him and that's just fine, but I have a huge problem with it.

Talk is cheap, people do what they want to do and all you have to is stand back and watch to see where their hearts are and what is important to them. They choose what they will do.

He is my person and he is the most important person in the world I live in. I can and will walk away from everything for him, to see him well, to help his life be better, to see him succeed.

I've looked at my so called friendships for the last two years. I've called a lot of people friend who have never given me their phone number or called me, who have never invited me to their house and have never been to mine. I have called a lot of people friend, but discovered they only love me when they see me and they were only friends because I called them that.

I'm not keeping score on anyone but I know just how excluded I've been. They've shown me who I am to them time and time again, I just kept hanging on out of habit and my own heart's commitments. The world is full of people, billions of them, one group does not change the entire big picture.

I know it sounds like I'm lumping everyone in together, but if the shoe fits wear it. My allegiance is to him, to my family, to my own life, just like their's is to their's. My sister tells me all the time, "You can't make anybody do anything" and she's so right, but people that don't do anything just don't fit into my picture.

There are so many people who talk the talk but don't do anything. You go to them for help and they offer prayer. You want them to show up for you and they don't, but you hear them call for you to show up for them.

With that being said, I'm walking away, I finding new people, I'm investing my time in my husband and my own life.

Everything that isn't real in your life will eventually weed itself out, you just have to recognize it and be strong enough to let it all go.

I am strong enough.

I will move forward.

I have no problem doing it alone.

Life just kept coming for me and I lived every moment of it.

I didn't know what I was going to do without a god in my world, I did a whole lot of things and I'm still living.

Aren't You Supposed To Be Loving And Witnessing To Everyone?

I've been being a good girl lately, posting positive and encouraging stuff, believing every word of it and then tonight I see a post that completely threw me off guard.

A "christian" group complaining about people adding atheist and devil worshipers to their ranks.

Seriously?

You have a problem with people you are supposed to be loving and looking like Jesus to?

You're already arguing with one another, so what's the difference in these guys being here?

Man!

What's wrong with people?

I'd rather get in a conversation with someone who doesn't believe in God and have the opportunity through grace and love to change their mind than get involved in the conversations that go on in these groups.

I've been purposely not participating in them because I don't want to get blocked from being able to post my videos and the message I'm putting out is important to the kingdom and others who are hurting. I'm purposely taking time off from social media to work on my painting, my studies, my positive energy, what kind of message I want to send the universe.

No one ever stops to think these people are probably the way they are because of how they've been treated by "christians."

How could they possibly believe in a loving God when His people display such a lack of it?

I wish I could say my mind is blown, but it's not. People don't surprise me anymore, their audacity doesn't either.

You're a child of God, you're supposed to be winning souls, right?

These are the people whose souls you are supposed to be winning!

Where's your love?

Whose your daddy?

Why do they not get included when God loves them as well?

I am a daughter of God, I am NOT a christian.

I love everyone like He loves me, especially the ones no one else wants to love.

I want to see everyone come into that same love and the example I set for others causes them to choose one way or the other.

I'd rather be love all the time and find out I'm wrong, than withhold it from a single hurting soul.

People are hurting, they've been wronged, life is happening to them and someone has to come along shining in their darkness!

Rant over.

Update: Today I know what phonies all of these people are and how they are as hateful as the god they think they believe in. I cannot believe I let people treat me the way I did.

I can't believe I argued over this god's existence for years, without evidence or proof that

he did in fact exist.

The #1 Source Of Disagreement On The Face Of The Planet

Oh my goodness!

There are days when I just don't get it!

It's like this horrible joke has been played on all of us and we fell for it.

Since we live in a world where blow dryers have tags on them telling you not to take a

bath with them, it is necessary for me to say right off the rip: don't get twisted up in what

I'm about to say.

I love my bible(s). They are my most prized possessions. There's the tried and true

New King James I've been carrying for the past fourteen years, the 400th anniversary

King James I've had for seven years, that's just as confusing as it ever was, but as

gorgeous as any hundred dollar bible would be. A new American Standard I just

purchased as my groovy little black preacher bible with the cross on the front of it.

There are several more scattered about the house, one a 1958 family bible, not my

family of course, but its one of my bibles nevertheless.

If I read, I read the bible.

It's an amazing book, full of death and horror and love and amazing stories of

deliverance.

It's also full of stubborn people who just can't seem to get it together and a God who

loves them but somehow seems to want to destroy them at the same time.

It's full of people no one else likes or thinks much of, but those are the people God chooses to be His great examples.

It's full of Jews, Greeks, Romans, Hebrews and Gentiles, whatever those are.

Some people actually think it's a baseball bat to beat everyone over the head with.

Those are the people who really do need to be beat over the head with it, literally..

Geez.

It's a book taken from oral teachings. It's full of history, poetry, metaphors, types, pictures and a whole bunch of stuff that already happened but they didn't write "The End" on the last page.

What's up with that?

Social media is covered up with discussions, debates and arguments over this book. There are those who will tell you it's the only way to Jesus. Ummm excuse me God doesn't need a book to reveal himself to people, He's God remember?

I read the book Tortured for Christ and Richard Wurmburg talked about a Russian soldier he met who loved Jesus. Later at the woman's house he discovered they had never even heard anything about Jesus, they just knew they loved Him.

Without the bible we wouldn't know who Jesus is.

I just don't whole heartedly buy into all of that.

I wasn't reading a bible when Jesus revealed Himself to me, I was smoking crack and jumping in and out of cars to get money.

Lately I've seen a lot of idolatry where it's concerned. The book is more valuable to people than the God being revealed in the book. They love the book more than the message and they hate anyone who disagrees with them.

Jesus is the word of God, not the bible.

There's no way God can live in a book, but there are those who will tell you that very thing.

Their every breath is hung on the words written in that book, not even understanding even a quarter of it.

People have tampered with it and let's be for real, they didn't talk that way during the period of King James, they played upon the colorful language of Shakespeare somewhere along the way. Atleast that's what I think they did.

It started out 80 chapters now its only 66.

Tell me no one has tampered with it again.

I know what the curse in it says, but Jesus destroyed all the curses at the cross right?

Men have tampered with it let's just be honest with ourselves about that one.

There are those who are so smart they've taken it apart, compared it with the history of that time and figured out it already happened. They can tell you things you never would have imagined because you've been sitting in a church pew eating up everything the pastor said, taking every word as truth, even if he was actually teaching it to you wrong.

Christians. I still think it was meant to sound derogatory, like a racial slur.

Their symbol is a torture device, the cross.

Christians eat their wounded, call everything good sin, accuse people of being witches, tell you "No no no that's not right, you can't do that you have to do this." They've hurt so many people there are those who want nothing to do with their god.

Their god is this small, bipolar, pissed off ogre sitting in the sky planning who he is going to smite next.

Their god is such a ego maniac he's going to burn you in eternal conscious torment in a place called hell that is not mentioned in the creation story and also appears as the home of the Greek and Roman god Hades in that people's mythology.

Do good go to heaven, do bad go to hell.

And if you don't agree with them you can go to hell too.

Madmen's logic.

The bible says......

The bible says.....

I've read it, I know what it says.

But Jesus talked about hell.

Jesus talked about a garbage dump outside the gates of Jerusalem where they threw the bodies of criminals and poor people, into the fires that were already burning, where worms ate everything they could.

If hell really existed, why isn't it in the creation story? It's all right there in the bible right?

They've also thrown in these dumb sayings that aren't in there, taking it upon themselves to speak for God.

God loves the sinner but hates the sin.

So dumb!

Jesus became sin on the cross, so we could become the righteousness of God and you want me to believe God hates Jesus?

Get a grip!

Why don't you be quiet and let God speak for Himself, because you're totally blowing it!

It's like they wrote it with a maze in mind. Hey let's throw this in there just so everyone will behave!

Lately I've had many conversations with God about it.

I'm like God, what's the point? It's almost like its tainted!

He never really says anything back about it, but I know He's not worried.

I read or I don't, doesn't matter to Him, because I talk to Him the rest of the time anyway.

I've been in the middle of reading and asked myself, "Why am I doing this? It's not about me, it never was."

For real, what's the point?

Some people can't even have a normal conversation with you about things, they have to make it all weird copying and pasting scripture in response to everything you are talking about.

I don't have all the answers and neither does anyone else.

All I do know is the gospel is good news, God is love, He remembers our sins no more, yet there's a parade of people all over screaming what He hates, how He's going to destroy their enemies, how you're going to hell if you don't love Him.

As far as I'm concerned it's all turned into total nonsense and a free for all for the haters.

There's so much beauty in it, a love story to top all love stories, but you wouldn't know that paying attention to social media and people who claim to know and love Him..

There are men and women in it who do amazing things, who are shown great love and forgiveness.

There's so much good that can be taken and applied to our lives, yet people's theology and doctrine is so dogmatic you'd never change their minds about it and what they believe about it.

Hell fire and brimstone preachers are still financially raping their congregations and teaching them fear based theology.

Scare the hell out of them rather than love the hell out of them.

Jesus is in there, there's no doubt about it, but men have been so ignorant for so long, passing down the same boogy man stories generation to generation that my heart has come to believe if they were all gone tomorrow we're left with love God and love others.

That alone would change the world overnight!

What if its all wrong?

What if we've all chosen to believe a lie?

I have questions people.

I don't just buy into everything people tell me, I'm from the streets, people can tell you anything they just can't tell you much.

I don't ride the amen train like the other religious zombies.

What if?

Right?

I love my quiet time when I'm reading but that moment comes along when I realize Jesus is in the room heavier than He was when I started and there's no reason to keep going.

We all love our own stories, but it's not our story, so what do you do with that?

Heard a lady tonight say God will destroy your enemies and then turned around in the same sentence and said He loves you.

I was like wait a minute. First of all I don't have any enemies for God to destroy because Jesus tells me to love them. And second I thought He was a creator not a destroyer and third listening to you He sounds like a bipolar psychopath serial killer!

But He loves me right?

Seriously?

Why would I want anything to do with Him?

Why oh why can't we get on the same page?

Who is responsible for this?

Were they all hallucinating only believing they were hearing from God?

I mean let's get for real here!

We're talking about men and haven't they been messing it up since the garden?

God is love and love cannot exist with hate.

Jesus taught love and didn't condemn anyone.

The bible is not the end all be all concerning your relationship with Jesus, because Jesus is the word of God.

I'm in a place where I have lots of questions and there are days when I walk past it with no intention of picking it up because I'm totally exhausted from being beat to hell with it all day long.

There's so much more I wish I had answers for but it is what it is and I find it totally amusing not one single person on the face of the planet really knows.

One thing is for sure it's the number one source of argument and misunderstanding.

The bible.

Update: I have zero respect for the bible. I still can't throw them away for some strange and twisted reason.

Everyone is still on the internet arguing about gods and all sorts of nonsense. I stay off the internet as much as I can because I don't care and I don't even want to see it.

Why I Am Not A Christian

If you know me and you read my blog what I'm about to say is not going to shake the very core of your belief system or make you wonder about me.

I am not a christian.

I know right?

I'm not a christian.

I have never been a christian and will never be a christian.

Why you ask?

Think about it.

Christianity - relating to or professing christianity or its teachings.

Do you see Jesus' name in there anywhere?

Neither did I.

Over the years its always made me uncomfortable when people asked me if I was a christian and maybe it was this deep buried belief of something closer to the truth.

Labels, labels, labels, we love our adjectives and to stick labels on everything.

Everything has to have a label right?

If I'm going to be labeled I'm going to label myself, but thanks anyway, you have fun with that.

When people ask me what I am, because they always ask you what you are, like one statement can define you (eyes rolling so far back in my head my brain tried to cover up), I always tell them I'm a Jesus Freak, or The Renegade of Grace, I'm Ride or Die or a Wild One. There are so many more I could use that would be totally funny and amusing, but these are the ones I trust.

I'm not a christian and proud of it.

I'm a child of the most high God, His precious and cherished daughter.

Christians were those people in the bible who followed Jesus and His teachings.

Try this on for size.

What if?

What if it was said for the first time like a racial slur? What if it was pronounced with disdain and hatred?

What if the term was never ever meant to sound anything but condescending?

What if the Pharisees hatred was so deep they said, "we'll call them christians, those fools! We'll show them!"

Let's face it, they don't look anything like Jesus.

People will tell you if you follow Jesus you have to be a christian, no hell no I don't!

Jesus lives inside me, so there's no following to be done, we are in union every moment of every day.

Christians was a term coined before the destruction of Jerusalem in 70AD, when all biblical prophecy was fulfilled.

It says they called them christians.

Who called them christians?

It doesn't say they called themselves christians, it says someone else did it.

Name calling seems to be a thing with people and I totally feel this is what was done.

"Those christians, they make me sick, they won't stop talking about Jesus."

Like really think about it!

It's mentioned three times in the new testament, but let's face it we're talking about the bible here. The book that paints God to be this destructive killing machine monster who sacrificed His own son, because He couldn't stand us.

The book that was written and edited and re-edited, and re-edited, then given to kings to pick out their favorite parts and lets not leave out the part where men are trying to control the behavior of others, rather than setting them free to know and love and understand the Father's heart.

Don't even think I'm beating up the bible, because I love the bible, but I don't have to agree with the way it's been used to hurt humanity and the brethren. I don't have to agree with all the wrong teaching, totally out of context, totally not about us and everything having happened already.

No rapture of the church, no hell, nothing the boogy men preachers of days long past taught and believe me when I tell you they couldn't have been more wrong. I'm sure Billy Graham was completely taken by surprise that he really didn't know, he just taught it the way others before him had taught it without question, because let's face it, we're talking about the bible here and men. Men have always tried to control one another and they have always used the bible to control the behavior of others from the very start.

When you look at the bible correctly, audience, time table, the events that actually took place, what is metaphorical and what isn't, you begin to see truths no one else has ever taught you.

I see academics every day all day long debating about it.

If you don't know what an academic is then you don't know one.

Anyway, I'm not a christian.

Truth be told you're not a christian.

None of us are christians.

We are sons and daughters.

We weren't born sinners because all those guys died back in 70AD, we were born children.

We're not Jews or even Gentiles.

We're not even the audience!

I'm a precious cherished daughter of God. I'm a beautiful warrior, a force to be reckoned with, a non-conformist, a heretic, a world changer, a lover of people, the list goes on and on, because no one word can define me. I'm not that girl that's going to jump on your "amen" train just because everyone else is doing. I'm not that girl you are going to tell what to do, because I'm not built that way.

I don't want to be like everyone else. I wasn't made from a cookie cutter, I am unique and there is no one else in the entire universe like me. You're not going to trick me into believing just anything and I'm pretty dang smart.

There's so much still to be understood, to be taught correctly, to change our minds about,

but this one thing I know for sure, I am not a christian and neither are you.

We are children, we have always been children and will always be children.

We cannot continue to write ourselves in the narrative of a book that isn't even about us

and never was.

We have to grow up, learn real truths, embrace what is truth for us and move on in love,

because people need love so much more than anything else.

I'm so greasy with grace and love and truth, your labels slip right off me anyway.

He already saved the world and now you're in it.

Now get in the pit and try to love someone.

Dope Dreams

If you've ever used drugs for any real length of time, you're going to have dope dreams.

Last night it was my husband, all messed up, staggering everywhere, his focus in a

million places at once and me dreading all the things that go along with that.

I had dope too, and a pipe, no lighter. Then I had a lighter, two pipes, more dope and he

wasn't there anymore.

The entire dream I want to get high but I don't want anyone to catch me or see me

getting high.

Room to room, situation to situation, still the dope is in my hand, the lighter in my

pocket and he's given me a pipe so loaded it's brown on the inside, even though it's no

longer than a cigarette butt.

I never did get high.

I never do in these dreams, the lighter is breaking, the pipes are falling apart, the dope

never gets smoked. I don't know how many of them I've had but the only one that I

almost got high in I was shaking so bad trying to light it, everything was shaking out of

the pipe and then I woke up.

Am I disturbed? No.

I don't get high anymore, I haven't gotten high in many years now and I don't want to get

high.

It's all just a trick of my mind, some filed away memories in my subconscious clearing out and making way for new ones.

I've never even had the desire to get high, though I've had thousands of thoughts about it, millions of images in my brain and memories over the years.

I don't struggle with it, I never have.

I know where al the dope boys live in two different states and still I don't care anything about getting high.

I've had long conversations with God to help me have more sympathy for others, because I don't understand why they still struggle.

I don't understand why my husband still struggles and I've been trying to figure it out going on seventeen years now.

The world is full of lies and it infuriates me to see the lies taught to others and to be told it's a disease and I'm going to die with it. Really? I can't tell. Why haven't I come down with it again, if it's a disease and can be caught? Recovery groups say, "Here let us help you but understand you're never going to be better." "Keep working it until it works", "Go to a meeting." I could go on and on with the nonsense I've seen taught, with the lies that have been told, with the false hope they pass out.

Why not just sit down and have a talk with your maker?

Why not take full responsibility for the choices you've made?

Why not decide it's not for you anymore and just don't do it?

I understand that it could quite possibly be different for every single person, but I don't understand struggling with it.

Had a friend that used to tell me to let the tape play out.

I let the tape play out until I didn't have to play it anymore.

It wasn't any fun and I'm a fun seeker.

So, letting the tape play out for me, is listening to that voice and letting that voice have more power than my own psyche. (Not happening.) Let's just say I did though.

Okay, so that voice is talking talking talking and ruining my concentration on everything else and I'm listening right?

Then the plotting begins, gotta have money, gotta have a person in mind to buy the dope from. Gotta have a lighter, the tools necessary to consume the poison and a place in mind to go and do it.

Believe it or not, I used to sit on the side of the street, at the bus stop, day or night, smoking, like it was legal, like no one could see me and to tell you the truth right this second my stomach is rolling around and bubbling and there's a huge darkness suspended in the air of my room

Let's say all those things fell into place and the person I bought the dope from really sold me dope and not something they made to look like it, because that happens as well. I knew a boy who constantly mixed goody powders to look like it and tricked people coming and going all the time, I've purchased $20 worth of dry wall flakes, after walking nearly a mile there and back.

Now what?

You get high and the minute you do that voice starts telling you you have to get more and that wasn't enough and it's on then.

The nightmare begins.

The tape continues to play, gotta get more, gotta get high.

The ending of that tape is me, jumping in and out of cars, no place to live, food would take my dope money, something to drink would take my dope money, sleep would stop me from getting high, scared to get I the next car, even though I need the money, because they might be the police or something even worse.

Nope.

Not doing it.

Been there done that, got the tshirt.

I am not going to die with this thing, you can't convince me to believe a lie.

I'm healed and whole and I don't care anything about it!

I go into the streets all the time, same people, same situations, they're getting high, the dope boys sometimes take plates.

It never crosses my mind.

I remember people in the trap, talking about how they'd been clean for such and such, I always ran into those at the end of their run, their family looking for them, they've pawned everything they've got with them, they've driven the dope boys around for days for crumbs, they are writing bad checks, overdrawing their bank account and somehow I've gotten stuck with them.

I remember one boy pulling his car into the middle of the park, in the middle of the night, then turning on the interior lights of the car! I'm gone!

I was the scariest white girl you've ever seen, paranoid, jumpy, impatient, would ditch you for the woods in the blink of an eye, turn money down all day long and drowning in misery.

The memory of that misery is what has kept me out the streets.

Pure unadulterated, want to die but don't have the courage to step in front of the bus, misery.

Thanks but no thanks, that's not for me

So, last night I had dope dreams.

Still I didn't get high.

People With Pitchforks And Torches

Not sure if anyone has noticed and don't really care if they have because I'm in that place, but I've ditched everyone.

Yes. I know, it's terrible, to stop being sociable, me of all people!

Anyway, I'm laying in bed tonight, should be asleep because I have to get up early in the morning and drive to Pine Level to take my grandson, DJ, to school.

Had a movie date night with my husband, something we haven't done in the last few weeks, because I paint and he plays video games.

I moved my painting out of the bedroom, so he could have the desk and the game console, because there isn't enough room in there for us both. It's really working out because I've produced more paintings over the last week than in the last three months and he's happy playing GTA and some of the internet platform stuff.

I've had nothing to say about any of it until tonight.

Me not having anything to say.

Yeah I know, it's not necessarily a good thing.

Anyway, life goes on and no one has really missed me because they are so busy with their own lives they haven't even noticed that I've been gone.

Yes, there are all these little religious sayings about people isolating, blah blah blah.

I'm focusing on what's important to me, that's my husband, my children, my home, my art and whatever else pleases me and gives me peace.

No one else takes care of that for me or can give that to me.

As for God, I don't want to hear about your God or their God or discuss what anyone actually thinks and believes about God, because what a freaking train wreck all of that is in the first place!

It's probably safe to say I've deconstructed religion to a point I think christians are merely more insane than the rest and I don't want to participate in their cognitive dissonance and the wrongly writing themselves into a two thousand year old narrative that doesn't have jack shit to do with them or anyone else. I've come to know some hard truths and who cares if you agree with me or not, I certainly don't and have come to a place where it's none of your damned business what I believe or don't believe and that's my right. It's between me and the being who created me and it's not based out of a book about first century Jews or the myths that it contains.

Before I go any further, everyone that knows me should know I still love them, I still value them, but for now this is where I am and this is where I will choose to remain and it's nothing personal toward anyone, it's just where I am.

I have a problem with excuses, beggars, victim mentality and anything that's fake. Anyone who really knows me knows this, it's just the way it is, it's how I'm hard wired. I've been through it and I'm tough as hell and although I try hard to be, I'm not nice all the time and I use the wonderful brain that's been deposited in my head and tough as I am, I'm not tough enough to be stupid.

That being said, I don't want to participate any longer, I don't need to be a part of, I accept myself, so I don't need other people's approval.

There's a man back there asleep in my bed who I think the world of, who I love simply because I love him. He's trying so hard to be what he thinks he should be, more than likely only because I love him and believe he can be anything he wants.

I don't expect anyone else to love him, he is mine.

I don't expect anything from anyone but I always live in great expectancy of wonderful things about to happen.

I'm freakin exhausted. I've planned parties, events, get togethers, street runs and you know what happens? No one shows up!

I invite others on every single adventure I ever have in mind, no one shows up.

I try selling things, to generate more cash for my household, no one responds.

I say what's on my mind and people accuse me of ragging everybody out.

I'm not hiding behind being nice right this second, I'm not using that super spiritual grace shield to tell a half truth about the state I'm in.

People suck, they are selfish, they don't give a shit about anyone but themselves and if you don't believe me just park your car on the side of the expressway and start calling people to see who shows up for you.

Everyone's heart is not the same. Some people talk a good talk but don't walk it. Some people aren't sober, they aren't doing their drug of choice any longer, hoping no one else notices and because I'm me and I know some things, people who are using anything they feel the slightest bit guilty about, they start avoiding me, because game recognizes game and God forbid anyone actually have some issues they aren't ashamed of or trying to cover up so no one else will see them.

Right this second, I'm done.

Screw everyone else's feelings for just a heart beat, what about me?

What about my feelings?

What about the hurts I've suffered at the hands of those I thought love me?

Yeah, screw them!

The one thing I've been telling him all this time is, "don't be ashamed and don't make excuses just own your shit."

I'm owning my shit.

I don't want to be a part of anything I feel is less than honest, less than truthful, less than what I would want to present to the entire world. Am I perfect or striving to be? Hell no! I will not go along with the status quo even if it kills me!

What about being honest and just saying what you really think?

Quit trying to dress everything up in nice-ness and just be you!

I'm over it! That's what I think!

I want to be loved all the time, not just because you saw me or ran into me somewhere!

I want to be valuable to everyone I meet, the same way they are valuable to me!

I've stepped away from everything and everyone and it's actually comical how no one has really noticed, because they are caught up in their own lives.

It's fine, I'm okay with it.

As for God, either He loves us all of He doesn't and it seems to me there's a lot of stuff He just really don't care about, because the church is in a two thousand year spiral of wrong teaching, wrong belief, and crucifixion over writings. Writings they don't really understand, that have been passed down pulpit to pulpit the wrong way until everyone is in a state of mind control and ignorance that reeks havoc on the rest of the world and leaves the poor scholars being beaten down by "God's people" and anyone that brings forth a good question or a new understanding of scripture is no better than the pagans they took half their traditions from.

Me personally, I'm painting, I love my husband, I love my family, I love everybody but I really don't give a flying rats ass what you believe or who your god is.

I don't have to worry about being left alone because I've never really been in company, definitely not one of the cool kids.

I feel so stupid for things I've said and done. I've called people my friends for years who I don't even have their phone numbers or have ever been invited to their house or out with them, who have never set foot in my own house or accepted my invitations. What kind of idiot does that?

Me, obviously.

I'm rebuilding from the ground up what I truly believe and if you don't mind I'm not going to share it with you, because it's not my intention to hurt anyone and you'd only attack me for it anyway, because isn't that the way it works? We destroy anyone who doesn't agree with us or believe the same things we do, never mind no two believe the same exact things in the first place.

I'm going to let it go at that.

Right now I believe I will go and crawl back into bed with my husband, the most important person in the world to me and I'm going to stop letting conversations roll around in my head, people take up space for free, situations affect me one way or the other. I'm going to edge in as close to his warm sleeping body and rest, with only hours before my alarm goes off.

Well You See What Had Happened Was

I was that girl, on fire for God. I had something to say, the thought of people who might want to hear what I had to say and years and years and years of constant bible reading.

I didn't even know what deconstruction was!

I'd never in my life heard the term preterism, never heard a whisper of Israel Only, or the Creating Christ Camp. I believe the latter rather than the former.

What do you do with all of it?

I'm going to be honest and just come out and say it I don't know anything anymore and I don't want to participate in the church circus because of it.

Indoctrination is like a slow poison, it seeps a little at a time, it is in no hurry to blend in and finish the job, it enjoys the suffering and the gasping for air.

There's an old saying that poison is a woman's weapon, funny how "the church" chose it. I see manipulation, lies, half truths, things that should have been said that weren't, the complete hijacking of the new testament by Paul and a god that for the life of me I can't figure out how people could ever come to believe is good and loving and all gummy bears inside.

I'm angry, I'm disconnected, I am exhausted and I really don't care to learn anything more at this time.

Hell, come to think of it I didn't even know what legalism was! All this garbage and confusion and dumb stuff that goes on centered around a book's teachings.

Saw someone ask how to present the cross to a bunch of little kids because it's Easter Sunday coming up.. Don't!

Good news is good news. It's good news all the time. Good news is full of good details. Good news does not contain details of murders and floods and crucifixions.

I cannot believe people have been so blinded and deceived about something that never had anything to do with them in the first dang place!

Get a grip people!

Man!

Here I am, I've been to church 3 times this year, have no desire to return anytime soon. I'm not mad at anyone and I love them all very much, I just can't stomach all of it any longer, because it's like the longest played prank in all of humanity, christianity.

Yeah I said it and you don't have to like it and I'm sorry if that offends you, but damn it, I always hated being the butt of someone's joke!

I left the streets and proceeded to lay my life down for everyone and every cause I could get my hands on and would still be doing that today had my support not run out.

I've come to a place where I want to lay my life down for my life! I'm laying my life down for my husband's life. I'm laying my life down for what's in my life! I've earned that, I deserve that and I don't really care who does or doesn't like it.

His life depends on it.

He's been locked up, rehabbed, taught about recovery, forced to attend meetings, still not getting real world skills from those places, so we're working what he knows. He has to be selfish about his sobriety and cannot deal with my madness. The first year is staying away from old places, old people, inside the bubble.

I don't want everybody knowing about it, I don't need to broadcast any of it and I'm protecting my privacy in a way I never have, not in my entire life.

I'm staying here, with him and if I go anywhere, it'll be with him and no I'm not co-dependent, or living in a fantasy world, or being controlled by anyone. I know who I am. I know where I've been and where I'm going, he either adds to my life or he doesn't, there's no need there, it's all just love.

I've drug that man to church everywhere, all the time, one time three different churches in one Sunday. I was going to church, didn't matter where I was, you better get your behind up and get ready for church and I fast on Sunday's, long time habit, don't ask me to make you breakfast, come on, we gotta go.

If he wants to lay up in my bed sleeping on Sunday mornings for the rest of his life, I don't care and

I'm not waking him to ask him if he's going with me.

I don't put on appearances for everyone, but I also don't want everyone in my business this time.

I'm on my own journey to whatever it is we all think we are trying to get to.

I've let go of all negativity concerning my disappointment with relationships, with those I just can't seem to connect with and those who were only pretending to begin with, for as long as it made them feel good. I'm avoiding a rare very few because I don't want to hurt them.

Hurt people hurt people and its just not necessary for those hurts to keep going around.

What's right in front of me is all I can deal with right this second.

I have a family right in front of me. I have a man who loves me who is trying to learn how to stop doing drugs right in front of me. I have a whole universe I secretly live in right in front of me. There's so much more right in front of me than a computer screen and every day life.

I want that.

I want to protect that, to nurture it and watch it grow.

I don't want anyone else's advice about it or their influence.

It's beautiful to say, it's beautiful to believe, but I have discovered, we are not in this together. There are factions and clicks and groups and the list goes on and on.

I have a precious few right in front of me and that's the only thing I want right now.

I see the arguments, debates over absolutely everything and I'm bored to freakin death by it all.

I want more from my life.

I want to do more, be more, learn more and expand my beliefs to the things my spirit has always rang true with that the ever watchful "church" discouraged me against, criticized and turned me off to by it's constant right and wrong banter.

If the Creating Christ camp is correct and my spirit feels like it is and don't give me that you can't trust your feelings bullshit, I'm from the streets and trusting my feelings kept me from getting killed many times, then it's the long played practical joke in all of human history and what a bunch of losers we really are for having believed those kinds of lies.

Don't make excuses for any of them! They knew what they were doing and still do! Billionaire pastors! Either God doesn't exist or He just doesn't give a shit.

Take your pick.

"His" people are the worst example of kindness and humanity I've ever witnessed and I used to be a crack addict. Drug addicts have more kindness and humanity for one another than "the christians" and they aren't slamming one another with stuff written in a book.

Screw you're being judgmental crap, I blogged it for a reason!

I want more.

This isn't good enough for me any longer.

I have to have more answers and I walk my talk, so you know I'll get those answers.

In the meantime I'm walking away from a church I spent the last nine years at. A place where I thought I was loved and valued. I've been to church three times this year when I probably didn't miss three times all of last year and eight people have hit me up wanting to know where I am. I was calling these folks my friends! I realized I've never been to their houses, I don't have their phone numbers, they don't invite my baby to the kiddy parties and what the hell is wrong with me? There are many I love and will always love and several I really am friends with, but that's just not where I want to be.

Everyone there is recovering addicts, including the pastor and no one give a shit past that?

Well, my husband came home the second week of January, not one soul has showed up over here to show him some love and we ran into a couple of them and they didn't even have the common courtesy to speak to him, when he was right there!

Oh I was given the whole "He needs to come to church" speech and I shot back with, "How about being the church and reaching out to him by coming by my place?"

Crickets.

Whatever.

I'm walking away.

I don't owe anyone an explanation.

How you love me is what I see not what you say just because you ran into me.

I'm owning my shit. I'm not accepting excuses at this time or any other.

My people just weren't my people and that's okay, my people are in their beds sleeping right this minute, I know them, they are a part of me, they want me in their lives and I am a priority. My people are as important if not more than all the people I've called myself helping over the years and that's where I'm focusing all my energy right now.

I don't want to be in the spotlight any longer.

I still love everyone.

I'm not going to be controlled and manipulated with love ever again, not even by my own husband, so people better figure that one out.

I have no answers about God at this point, either He's there or He isn't, that's all I've got.

The Deconstruction Of Darlene

Over the last year or so I've come to a new place in my journey.

I friended someone on social media who taught me how to ask questions, how to look for answers, how to use my own brain concerning spiritual matters and God.

By the way the picture is of the street corner I used to buy drugs on and prostituted from. I've been keeping it to myself for many reasons but mostly because it is mine and mine alone and I didn't want to share it with anyone until I was sure where I stood concerning everything religious.

Lines are going to be drawn, people who I thought were my friends are going to reject me and walk away, others have already done so.

My husband came home for the first time in almost two years in January and before he arrived I made a decision to walk away from everything and dedicate my time and energy to his wellness. So far so good. He's working, has some clean time, is selfishly protecting his sobriety and I'm okay with that.

First it was Preterism and the belief that all events mentioned in the bible has already been fulfilled and is finished.

Then I moved into the Israel Only camp. Israel only is the text being only about the tribe of Israel and dealing with their story and their God. Matthew 15 24 says and Jesus said to her I have only come for the lost tribe of Israel. I still believe a large portion of both.

I met someone else who asks the best questions and assured me if I thought I had an experience with God, then I had an experience with God and no one could discredit or discount that belief.

I still believe I had an experience with God, but I no longer need that belief to live my life and identify myself with.

Along the way I began to observe those who said they love me. I began to watch what others did who claimed to love God.

It was a very lonely and confusing place for a little while.

Relationships I had began to fall apart, not because of my belief but because people just don't do things for long. They do what makes them feel good until it doesn't make them feel good any longer.

Truth be told I set some of them up, just to see where their hearts were and stood back to watch.

I'd like to say they came through for me, but that is not the case.

I've actually found a flaw in their grace message. Grace people don't have to show up because they are free and because they are free they mostly don't show up.

It's been almost five months now, haven't been to church, heard from a hand full of people and I mean a hand full. (The pastor, his wife, his mother who is my best friend, a girlfriend or two.) All those other people who said they loved me every Sunday they saw me, not even an "I miss you,", or "why haven't you been to church?" message.

Not one single man has reached out to my husband and they all used to be drug addicts themselves.

Anyway, so what? Who cares? My life didn't revolve around any of them in the first place, they were just a part of it and I gave way too much allegiance to them and not enough to him until now.

During that time I began to ask my own questions, dig for my own answers and reject their message of love and grace altogether. "We're in this together." No we are NOT. I'm in this with my husband and him alone. "We show up for one another." No hell you do NOT, because I remember specifically asking and everyone went ghost and now they are no longer welcome.

I roamed around in the rooms, learning, trying to figure some things out, watching the academics and scholars argue just like "the christians" and then something new and wonderful and eye opening happened. A historian produced another theory to consider and that was it for me. My spirit screams every day it's true and I really don't care who believes me or agrees, never did in the first place.

I am in the myth camp, now and forever. It's all a myth and you will never ever convince me that a copyright rip off religion has a true and living character attached to it.

Why? You might ask.

I believe it that's why.

I don't buy into the bible says the bible says rhetoric and never did. I always operated out of a place of love that was my own, still is my own and will remain my own for all of my life. I don't need a god or a religion or even a belief system to be who I am, to love like I do.

Jesus is a myth, just like all the other gods in religion.

With that being said you can keep your persecution and accusations and all your little religious sayings and threats because I have never ridden the proverbial amen train and I never will. Hell, I lived in a tent in the woods on Fulton Industrial Boulevard for three years, I'm not scared of anything.

Ignorance may be bliss but not for me. I want more, have to know more, I'm sick of this religion eating it's wounded and destroying anyone in it's path that doesn't agree.

God is love.

Yeah okay.

Where's that love in the world amongst his people, hard as hell to find that's where.

Those who remain in my life are those people, the ones who really love, who can do that past their religion, who were absolutely wonderful and loving from birth.

If you need a god to be loving then you're just a shit head to begin with.

I'm never turning back, I don't care what anyone thinks or says, they don't have to live my life, they don't even want to be a part of it in the first place, so whatever!

What I believe and what I can prove are two different things, but the burden of proof actually lies on the people who buy into the bullshit.

I have deconstructed to my own truths, I have gone off the deep end and used my own brain and I will never ever return to the beliefs I once held true.

Think about it. A book that has nothing to do with anyone living today, the scholars still haven't completely figured out, everyone has argued over for two thousand years. It's full of metaphors, poetry, myths, legends and you want me to believe the central character is real? Get the hell outta here. Do you hear how crazy that actually sounds? The Romans created it, they always hijacked other people's religions, they had a holy war on their hands and people were already looking for a savior. They gave them a passive, turn the others cheek, love your enemy, hang out with those no one else loves messiah. It's a great message but it's a myth, just like the character it's built around. There are no writings by Jesus and he was not illiterate according to the text. Everyone else was writing, but not him. Yeah okay.

I'm not even going to go into all of it, because it would absolutely take weeks and months and years to unpack it all for you.

I encourage you to ask questions, to begin using your own brain, shake the indoctrination off and use some damned logic for a change! Snakes don't talk, donkeys don't talk, no one ever lived inside the belly of a fish for three days and Jesus is a myth. They can prove all these others lived but not him? Myth.

I don't care what people will say, most won't even be surprised because they really know me as a person and I'm always full of surprises and liable to say anything at any give moment in the first place!

Most will dismiss me, others will attack me, others still will walk away, but there will be one or two who trust me enough to accept the challenge of finding their own answers, asking their own questions and still love me regardless.

Do I still believe there is a God?

Yes.

What kind of God, a passive, doesn't interfere should love his creation so much more

God and with children starving to death in Africa he's still suspect..

I don't know, I just know I never did and I never will drink the kool aid.

I love you all so much.

What I believe should not affect your love for me but if it does, rock on, you really

didn't love me in the first place and we both know it.

Darlene's religious beliefs have left the building.

There Is Only Now There Is Only This

In getting in tune to who I am, what I want and the energy I possess, I've been stepping
back from social media, from things that cause me to worry, from activities that may
cause resistance or negative feelings.

Social media is the absolute worst for this!

Yesterday, I wasn't really participating but the computer was sitting right next to me as I
was painting and a post popped up. This young man was slamming someone else who
unfriended him, because the two were wasting extensive energy arguing over religion.
The post was made in a mocking way asking others how laughable was it.

I pointed out it was a laughable as his slamming the guy for everyone to see because
they didn't believe alike.

He kept trying to draw me into the narrative and overlooking the statement I made.

I let him know I really didn't care about the conversation or the content of it and stated
how he came to a place where it was okay for him to slam the guy publicly over their
difference of opinion.

Not once did he see his part he played in it and because he couldn't draw me into it he
began slamming me!

Needless to say I unfriended him and didn't let it go any further, because that's not where
I am today.

I'm not going to let some knucklehead get into my energy field and throw me off when

I'm creating such a beautiful life for myself. The days of letting others knock me off my track are over. I love them but I don't care what they think and religion is the most negative subject anyone could ever bring up, because all anyone ever does is argue about it.

I've even been recently attacked for my lighthearted jabs at it.

I've been told all sorts of horrible things about myself because I've chosen not to participate in that madness any longer and its just so disheartening that people have begun to be so unkind to one another over differences of opinion.

I am an original and who I am is appreciated and loved by my creator and others have no part in that, it's between the two of us.

As time goes on you'll see me participate less and less because my focus is in putting the positive energy out and ignoring the negative or getting rid of it all together.

I am a creator and I will not create that which isn't beneficial to myself and others.

I don't have to be and don't want to be like everyone else, because I am not like everyone else and I have a different purpose to serve than others do and that's okay.

I will not waste my precious energy on activities, conversations, or people who throw shade and negativity everywhere they go.

It's a new day in my life and my life is going to be amazing and full of wonder and exciting happenings from now on. I cannot entertain any sort of negativity whatsoever! It's such a waste of time and energy. There is enough right in front of me that I don't need anyone's approval or even a pat on the back, I create my world, my life is mine and mind alone.

Stop giving your energy to vampires!

Stop participating in the negativity of the world, this includes religion and discussions of it.

It's counter productive to creating, it doesn't make you feel good and it's not any fun, so why do you do it?

I'm not doing it anymore!

Believe whatever the hell you like about whatever you like, it doesn't matter to me and you're not going to draw me into the narrative. Truth is simply something someone gave attention to.

My truth is I don't care any longer and I won't begin to care ever again.

My truth is there is more to have, to do, to be, to create and that's where my focus is.

My truth is a life waiting for me somewhere else and a house full of blank canvas to fill before getting there.

My truth is I am able to walk away and never look back and that's exactly what I'm going to do because where I am going is in front of me. It's full of happiness and harmony and fun and the expectancy of miracles every single day.

You can have that other stuff, I don't want it anymore and it was never was mine to start with.

I'm staying in my vibration and anyone who doesn't vibe with me simply has to go and it's very personal.

We spend our lives thinking of the things we don't want and because of that we attract those very things.

I'm thinking of the things I do want and I'm attracting those things every moment of every day and those things do not include mindless, heartless people who beat everyone down because of the differences in opinions they have with one another.

It's a beautiful life, there so much left to create, why would you waste another second of it involving yourself with things that don't matter, that don't improve the quality of your life and in the end leave you angry, frustrated and sad with people who don't give a rats ass about you in the first place!

With that being said, let me say this.

I love you but I don't care what you think about me.

That is all that matters.

It is a higher vibration.

It's the beauty of my life and all that is in it.

Osho said the greatest fear is the opinions of others.

I can't use someone else's opinion.

She Was Sleeping On The Sidewalk

We're leaving the Varsity, going to get on the highway and I see this woman sleeping on the sidewalk, right next to the street, traffic everywhere.

I saw lots of people in the street today, my people, people who didn't even know my heart recognized them. A lady with her jeans tied with a boot lace, that wild look in her eye. A man who could barely walk carrying a couple of bags, I saw sitting on a bench as we drove back through.

A guy sitting on an overpass wall, intently writing something in a book.

People sleeping against the walls, people's stuff, shopping carts, a bag lady with her dog who had lovely dreds.

I saw them. I saw each and every one of them. They were not unnoticed today, not one single one of them.

I searched for them as I drove along, knowing they were there.

It was overwhelming.

It's easy to be a big fish in a little pond, but what about making an impact in the ocean without growing any bigger?

I put them in my memory, make sure the burn is deep, so I never ever forget them. I carry them with me in my love for them.

Everywhere I go I see homeless people.

My heart is so broken that I can't help them all but I guarantee you I will love those He's given to me enough for all of them.

I will love them for the rest of my life.

And I'm crying..

Sunday

Tomorrow is the big day!

The day I wait for all week long.

The day my heart is wrapped around.

Sunday!

Woot woot!

I can hardly wait!

Gonna get loud!

Get my praise on!

After that, more good stuff.

Pick up the food, back to the house.

Get it ready and go see our folks!

Who Cares If They Don't Show Up?

Ever get the feeling you are the only one standing in the stadium?

Ever feel like you are the only one who cares?

Over the last year I've grown a great deal and an area in my life God has been working on is other people.

If you want to do something just do it. Invite others to go, the real ones will show and life keeps moving.

I have this over reaching mind that has the most tremendous dreams and expectancy. I see countless faces in these fantasies. I believe everything can turn big.

I just keep going, keep doing, keep being.

At the end of the day its just Jesus and me anyway.

Is it disappointing? Well of course it is! We all want people to come along, we were created for community, not isolation.

I've got the courage to just keep going, with or without anyone else. It's always Jesus and me anyway.

Who cares if they don't show up?

They are the ones missing out.

You still get to do exactly what you were called to.

Don't stop inviting them, because some day they may surprise you and don't be discouraged, you've got enough to do it on your own.

Update: I cared if they didn't show up and they didn't show up more than they did.

So many things I planned and people said they would be there. So many times I stood there all alone, my heart broken, disappointed with everyone.

People make time for and do what they want to do, if it's not important to them they don't show up.

I learned quickly it wasn't important to them and neither was I.

Let's Love The Dumb Out Of The Church

Like I've said before, I am friends with several academics.

The definition of academic is 1.of and or relating to education and scholarship. 2. not

of practical relevance, of only theoretical interest

Academics are people who are so smart their brains just don't work like everyone else's.

My friend Randy, was an academic. He used to be the computer professor at Georgia

Tech, his ex wife works for the CDC, their children are immensely intelligent.

He's written me a composition about how the tribe of Israel committed genocide and it

was so complicated I had to have a dictionary to look up words to understand what the

heck he was talking about. Yet, I had to walk him through Facebook on the phone,

because it was so simple he couldn't figure it out.

Yesterday I watched a video by one of these such people and he was talking about

discrepancies in the bible. The mention of scripture in one place mentioning it being

said in another and it appearing no where in said scripture. One priest's name used when

it was actually another priest who held the office as the time those things happened.

These people absolutely amaze me, teach me something new every single day and reveal

to me a knowledge of scripture I never had before. Stuff so deep yet so simple I can't

understand why it all hasn't made sense before now.

These friends of mine put up the most stunning thoughts about God, things that really

make you step back and challenge every single thing you've ever been taught, because believe me when I tell you it's been taught completely wrong to a lot of people, for a very long time.

Good Lord!

I thought God and Jesus and the Holy Spirit were three separate entities until I was grown, because no one took the time to explain this, they were too busy preaching hell fire and brimstone!

When my friend Lucy explained it to me and helped me to see Him better, my mind was blown!

No one ever taught me that!

No one ever told me Jesus loved me and nothing could separate me from His love. I was raised in the bad God, good Jesus generation of wrongly taught people. Turn or burn! "They're all headed to hell......", "God loves you but......", "Your best is as filthy rags."

Then came the stupid stuff.

Do you know where you're going if you die tonight?

Did you lead them in the sinner's prayer?

If you'll take one step He'll take two.

Love the sinner, hate the sin.

How could a people hand picked by God from the foundation of the world be so dumb and ignorant?

If you'll sew a seed, you'll reap a harvest.

Give and it shall be given to you, pressed down and running over.

Lies told for so long and so loudly, generations of men carrying the same lies and dumb church sayings?

Why?

Why take something so beautiful and twist it up to control others?

Why lead people to slaughter with judgement and condemnation.

When I was a kid, going to church, growing up in the church, I always felt terrible, wondered if I would ever be good enough to make it, without ever knowing I had believed a lie.

I was a wretch, a filthy sinner, how could God possibly love someone like me?

Jesus sets you free!

Oh but wait, you must be saved.

You must repent of your sins and pick up your cross.

You must die to self daily.

Nero burned christians in his garden as torches.

The christians are the ones carrying the torches now.

No matter how many religions there are, what people think about God, their god, or other people's gods. There are really only two divisions and isn't it sad there is division in the body?

Those who believe God unto salvation, that its a free gift, it can't be earned and nothing can separate us from His love. His love is unconditional, it doesn't change with our behavior, whether it be good or bad.

Then there are those who don't believe us.

They are a vehement as hungry snakes.

They attack every new idea they could possibly have with the lies they've been taught since they first heard about Jesus.

They attack those they don't agree with.

You couldn't possibly know Jesus, you need to repent.

All of a sudden this person is making assumptions, throwing out accusations, beating you over the head with scripture and telling you all about yourself from somewhere else in the world, on the other side of a keyboard. A christian, a brother or sister. Someone who doesn't know you from Adam!

Damning you to hell because they don't like your ideology .

This madness takes them over and they go nuts with it. They take it to the extreme.

They begin to twist what you said and making assumptions about it and you. They have to have the last word about how horrible you are and God couldn't possibly love you. It's so dumb.

It used to make me mad, still does frustrate me sometimes, but in the end it makes me sad they are so blind and lost and miserable they have to come along and beat up on me for a while. If they were drowning and I was there to save them, they wouldn't take my hand and just drown, they are that determined to disagree.

I don't block people like I used to, but lately I'm having to put repeat offenders on the list and they won't be coming back off it. This one guy in particular kept coming after me, again and again and again.

Most of these rooms are think tanks. The statements being made are for great thought and insight, not controversy. The people in these rooms are expected to be of a certain intelligence and open mindedness.

God's people have been hard headed and hard hearted from the start, I don't know why it still surprises me today.

We've all been slighted or assaulted by one of these God fearing bible thumping people and half the time even they don't know what they are talking about.

It's a comedy of errors.

I've encountered more of these people in that last year than ever before, mean nasty hateful people who claim they love God.

Really?

Seriously?

Cause I can't tell buddy.

God's really been dealing with me about them and giving me lots of practice being persecuted by them.

I'm getting much better at it.

There are times during the courses of these conversations when I simply say things like "Jesus is amazing!" something contrary to what I really want to say.

Jesus is the game changer.

His love saves the world.

Jesus loves you.

Lots of times these simple beautiful statements shut them down.

Then there are those who just have to have the last word.

They aren't going to stop no matter what.

Other times I keep moving and say nothing at all.

You can't tell a fool anything.

I know because I used to be one.

There are days when I am so discouraged and frustrated I want to scream and I'm sure my eyes have awesome muscles from rolling them so much.

Those are the times I have to remind myself Jesus loves them too, even in their stupidity.

Love wins.

Love doesn't attack others, or have to be right.

Love doesn't tell someone all about themself and condemn.

Love.

Show them love.

I know they're dumb as a truck load of bricks, but they can't help it, they've been wrongly taught.

They don't have the freedom of heart and mind to understand the mysteries yet.

They've been chained to a mixed message of half truths and rules their entire lives.

They don't know any better.

I know for a fact I've embraced many lies in my life.

When the truth about Jesus' love for me was revealed, no one would ever be able to lie to me again, and expect me to believe them.

I know who I am. People are always going to talk, some of what they say is true.

At the end of the day, none of this matters, it's Jesus and me. It's my Daddy, the creator of the universe loving on me, having a relationship with me and all the bibles in the world couldn't even begin to describe what that's like! That's an experience for me and me alone, being with Him.

I love to learn but how much of it is really necessary?

I love Him.

He's so much more than anyone could ever even find the words for.

He created the universe! Let's get for real on this one!

Be patient with others, you don't know what their struggles are.

Walk away from disagreements, because no one wins.

Pray for those who curse you.

Love your enemies.

These people aren't supposed to be our enemies, they are supposed to be our brothers and sisters.

Loving people and being a gold digger I know there's some good in there, I just can't see it past their fear. Fear has two responses either fight or flight, these folks are looking to fight.

They've been beaten down with lies and half truths for so long, they believe all of it and you're crazy if you don't. They've probably been hurt, a lot. Hurt people hurt people right? We always kill that which we don't understand. There is good in there, Jesus loves them.

It's hard to see that when they are beating and kicking me down, but I can take it, I'm a tough cookie.

When ever you are given the choice to be right or be kind, always choose being kind it's going to get you so much further with absolutely everyone.

Billy Graham just passed and he was what they say he was, but I can't sit through an entire sermon of his without cringing half a million times because it's so evident he believed the lies that were handed down by preacher after preacher. I can't receive any of the things he's talking about because he was seeing through a lens of distortion.

Do I think he loved Jesus?

Of course I think he loved Jesus.

Do I think his message was one God wanted going out into the nations?

You'll have to ask the Big Guy about that one, it was between them.

One thing is for sure, I've got a better message and so do all the people I'm running with.

I don't care what anyone tells you, nothing can separate you from His love.

At the end of the day it's just you and Him.

You and God and nothing else matters.

His love is not affected by your behavior, He's not a love me or else kind of God.

Rather than arguing begin to pray for these people every time you encounter them.

 Begin to bless them to know the truth.

Leave them and let God sort them out.

They are His masterpiece just like you.

Let's love the dumb out of the church.

NEVER HAPPEN!

You already know I was going through some stuff, it's messed up. I was betrayed, shunned, lied to and now no one likes me because I did the research and have no reason to believe in their god.

I don't even make it weird for folks, but they sure the hell do for me.

Man oh man was I going through something.

I thought all those things were truths just like the people who think they are truths today.

I can't find any truth in any of it any longer. There never was any truth in it to begin with. Gods are created by men, not the other way around.

Lover's Lane

Today is the day!

This afternoon we're taking it to the streets with beautiful love letters written on poster board.

Signs that say things like "Jesus loves you,", "God's not mad at you,", you know!

Beautiful words of love for those driving by to see.

It's one hour every other Saturday.

It's going to be amazing and anyone can do it anywhere they live!

What if? All the people I've been talking to, all over the country, did the same thing?

What if? So many of us did it in so many different places the news would start getting a hold of it!

What if? We all showed up!

What if? God made the entire thing go viral!

That would be so awesome!

Too many times you see folks with signs that have no good news. Signs yelling warnings and telling you you're going to hell if you don't repent.

Who came up with this nonsense?

Who decided the people should be controlled with fearl

What knucklehead rejected the good news to lead people in another direction.

I've seen these signs.

They are horrible, they are an assault to the senses and they lack love in the most extreme ways.

Think about it! Give a choice, which would you choose? Turn or burn? Or Jesus loves you?

I'll take the good news! Jesus loves me!

All you have to do is google "christians with signs" and there you have it! It's like a b-rated horror flick of folks claiming to love God but the signs they are sharing with others lack love, kindness and grace.

The gospel is supposed to be attractive, we are supposed to make it attractive with our love.

Evangelist have turned off generations of would be followers with these horrible signs. Signs spewing condemnation and judgement.

I love the one at gay pride, the guy standing there dressed like Jesus with a sign that reads, "I'm not with these guys." All around him are these statements of pure hatred, from folks who are supposed to be God's people.

I want to turn the tides on street preaching and so many that have come before us actually turning people away rather than catching them.

Jesus said to follow Him and He would make us fishers of men.

Some people's bait smells bad and should have never been dropped into the water.

You can't scare the hell out of people, you have to love the hell out of them. Perfect love casts out all fear.

If you would like to participate you can do it anywhere! You can make your own signs, full of love and hope, of course, pick somewhere to go stand with them and wave and smile at all the traffic going by.

It's easy.

I plan all sorts of things, try pulling huge numbers of people together, believe that every plan I have has the ability to grow to fill stadiums. That's the eternal hope God has planted in me, expectancy that something wonderful is about to happen, that anything could happen and for sure something is going to happen.

I told my people I'm not scared to stand out there and do it by myself.

Let's be love today.

Let's save lives today.

Let's look like Jesus everywhere we go!

Two o'clock! Meet me at the fountain in Prattville!

If you're doing it, please take pictures and share them with me, that would be totally awesome.

I love you all so much!

Today is going to be a great day.

Lover's lane!

Update: The problem with church folks is they love to do stuff, as long as it makes them feel good. I was the only one that stuck to the things I did, made a commitment to all of

it.

You Are Not Alone

I made the appointment today. Why?

There was a time in my life when I was very mentally ill.

I'm seeing things I clearly remember from then, I'm having trouble controlling my emotions, my depression is way beyond the normal ups and downs of every day life and crying for nearly a week when no one else is around or while working is a clear sign something may or may not be going on.

Better to err on the side of caution.

I've been well for such a long time, I'm so thankful for that.

I remember certain things about that time very clearly, days when I felt like I could do anything and I was so up in the air I made everyone around me nervous. Then came the depression. I once spent an entire week on the couch, went to see the psychologist wearing the same clothes I'd had on the week before: not good.

This was a red flag for me.

It's not a hygiene issue, it's something else. I've noticed this lately, the same clothes from the day before. I've noticed the crying isn't my usual, I've noticed the thoughts. I don't want to talk about the thoughts I've been having because I don't want anyone to freak out. Thank God I'm not hearing voices, at this time.

I'm under a great deal of stress with my job. I have been here four years and it's sad to say, but every single day I feel like I should be packing my stuff and looking for a job.

My boss has a way of making me feel like I'm a total failure and she doesn't respect me and getting fired would land me in the streets.

My brother called me today and I told him I'd made an appointment because I felt like I might be having some issues, he simply said, "shit." They all remember how bad it was, how out of control I appeared to be, the madness that followed and my going to prison. I'm not ashamed to talk about it because not talking about it could very well kill me.

I'm not complaining or trying to dump my problems at anyone else's door, but I know there are those out there who think no one understands. I'm being transparent and putting it there so someone, anyone, can feel like they aren't the only one.

I want others to know so they can reach out, invite me to reach out and to encourage those who feel they are traveling through a world of darkness. We are in this together right?

It's not the end of the world, I promise. It's another challenge to make me grow, to stretch me and to use my pain as a platform.

Yes I am that girl.

I will not be defeated.

Your pain can be a prison or a platform. I've learned sharing it makes it less powerful, causes it to lose it's grip on me and my heart is always geared toward helping others and encouraging the world at large.

If you're struggling with mental illness, you are not alone and you don't have to go it alone. There are so many resources, places that will work with you on a sliding scale, people who would love for you to reach out to them and even more still willing to lend an ear or good advice. Don't go it alone!

It's okay to be broken, God uses broken vessels all the time, doesn't stop your light from shining through the cracks.

I have a mental illness, but it doesn't have me. My brain is broken, but I am whole in Jesus.

Update: I totally want to throw up. I'm still mentally ill, as a matter of fact I am still very mentally ill, but it's much better than indoctrination and I'm educated about it the same way I'm educated about religion and writings. It's so sad this is where I was, knowing what I know today.

Religion

I came out of religion a little over a year ago.

Some people hurt me. Some let me see who they really were and how fake that was.

Some people still love me we just are no longer connected. I have two girlfriends and a neighbor. Virtual girlfriends in the hundreds, all types, beliefs and walks.

There's an old joke that everyone who is an addicted gets religion in some form when they stop doing drugs.

I met a guy and he told me what full prctcrism was.

He taught me to ask questions.

He calmly and thoroughly took it all apart and put it on display for everyone to see.

He is a force of calm.

He asks questions.

He has no emotional investment in any of it.

I'm emotional.

I hate religion.

I despise the things people say to me when I tell them I'm a myth camp atheist.

I had never looked at it that way.

What did I really believe?

Was there really a god?

Who had I spent the last eighteen years of my life talking to?

What the hell?

Let's just say I studied and copy and pasted my way out of it.

I am learning to ask questions simply for the sole purpose of being an asshole and it being a really dumb question.

Anyone that knows me will tell you, I studied the bible nonstop for well over thirteen years. Day and night, night and day, even at work. Don't try to tell me shit about the bible. I know the bible.

It's all so ridiculous.

People arguing over who has the best imaginary friend.

Adults have gods.

I was super hurt and destroyed and at a huge loss at first. I cried alot. I was angry about a whole world of things. People kept saying the same stupid shit they say every day over and over again, like a broken ass record.

It there was a god, his need for an instructional manual immediately tells me he doesn't have his shit together.

Not only that but an instruction manual that no freaking body understands or can agree upon.

They use forgeries. LOL. Yes forgeries. Imagine that. Several of the Pauline epistles are proven forgeries.

What does forgery mean to you?

Means dude didn't write it and there is a deception there and why would you still use something of that nature to represent your religion?

A guy that never mentions your savior?

And your savior.

Let's address that guy.

Jesus.

Not one single writing.

No more than a story about etching in the sand.

Get the fuck out of here.

Think about it.

The biggest guy in the whole freakin religion, in a time when they are all writing things down, talking about things in scrolls. Not one? Seriously? Not one. He's the guy, but he didn't write anything?

Aight.

Emperors called themselves and made others treat them as gods. This guy is a god and was here and didn't write anything. They were all writing stuff.

Anyway.

I am not religious any more. I don't want to talk about it. I don't care about it. I have a life that is just as good without it as it ever was with it.

The people who hang around with me and participate in my life are the ones who really love me and there's little time outside of them and their value.

You can have your god.

I don't want him.

He's all your's.

Enjoy

It Was Nice Knowing You

This is not a ploy for attention. It's not a post where I expect any feed back or anyone to throw in what they think.

I've been struggling with social media for a couple of years now.

It started with a video that had Jesus in the title and it's only gotten worse.

Now it's 30 days facebook jail every 30 days.

They've crippled my ability to do business through yard sale sites.

I'm sure I've lost a lot of friends over the past couple of years, deconstructing to the point of atheism.

It's okay. I don't mind. I didn't ask anyone what they thought or to weigh in in the first place.

I have given it considerable thought over the last three months.

I can't use all the negativity.

I see constant fear, worry, people talking about things they don't know anything about, others chiming in to tell them they are wrong and half the time those people don't know what they are talking about either.

I see people learn new things and others make fun of them for it.

I see people crying out for help and no one is paying attention to them, because everyone is so wrapped up in their own junk they are oblivious to the existence of anyone else.

Selfies. What's on your mind?

Current events have folks straight losing their minds and forgetting who they really are. For every good post there are twenty more that are negative. For every good post there are a hundred more talking about the same damn thing.

For every person that puts out a positive vibe, there's some shit head lurking in their friends section, just waiting for the opportunity to make his or her smart ass comment, who really don't like you anyway.

I see people talking shit about people they don't even know. Talking shit about people who haven't done a damn thing to them.

I see the passive aggressive bullshit the real cowards put out. I see the narcissist who is pouring salt on everybody, trying to one up everybody they know, name drop, be somebody. No one has told him you can't do those things using everyone else as stairs. I see politics, us verses them, lines of division, religion, racism, all sorts of things going on in the world.

Not only that, you have to support those people or they start calling you out on social media.

I see you're not free to do whatever you want, because you are supposed to consider my health and my feelings first.

If you're not this, or you're not that, you ain't shit. It's like a real time magazine. Magazines always make you feel like shit about your life and your house and what you look like and the clothes you wear. They offer all this advice you didn't ask for and you start believing that nonsense. Sound familiar?

I see people standing around making videos of other people being mistreated and no one saying a word to interfere or make it stop. I see people standing in front of burning buildings with their phones stuck in their faces.

I see people judging me for what I don't believe, for what I do believe, for not being like them, for not believing in the same things they believe.

I see people judging one another for absolutely everything else.

I see racism being fed and nourished and coddled by people like an old friend.

I know my life doesn't matter because I'm not black.

I am painfully aware of what color our skin is thanks to you and all your little friends.

I am painfully aware how something someone else did to other people is supposed to have everything to do with me here and today and I should be punished for all that wickedness.

I am painfully aware how you have attached your identity to it and continue to draw the lines, to choose sides, to use the language and rhetoric that keeps us divided.

I am painfully aware how my human experience couldn't possibly measure up to anyone else's because of some stupid ass invisible privilege they believe there is.

Believing in white privilege is like believing in Jesus, I'm not buying your bullshit on either one.

I was born poor, to an abusive father, in a world that didn't let me choose, a convict's daughter, so fuck you and your white privilege bullshit.

I'm divorcing a black man who has been arrested 32 times, it's not a black white issue, it's shitty people carrying badges. It's people not using good sense in tense situations. It's not being compliant with a person that's already on edge. It's not being completely honest for the sake of your life.

The world is not coming to an end.

Even if it did no god is coming to save you.

I try putting out a good message all the time. I'm not perfect, I have moments when it all pisses me off and I want to say something about it too. It's just too much.

For all the good it could do in the world it does nothing more than feed the negativity. You'll see blog posts, pictures, things I have for sale, but other than that, I can't and won't participate.

I've been writing and painting and just living my life and every day without it makes my life so much more lovely, because it's negative, it's a slow poison, it's not benefiting my soul one way or the other. It's a constant back and forth of ideas and beliefs and arguments.

People can say things to you so vile you want to go and shower, but the moment you respond.......

There's no free speech on social media.

Artificial intelligence is running the whole show now and if you're on the list, ,then you're on the list and the list doesn't discriminate. The program runs the way it's designed to run and they are just racking up points on you for the next time they shut you out and shut you up.

I am returning to life as we once knew it. I'm working, I'm gardening, I'm house shopping and the whole world really doesn't give a shit, so no one needs to know it. I've had a dozen people out of nearly five thousand reach out to me in the last ninety days and that tells me everything I already know about social media.

Out of sight out of mind.

I've just finished my second book and am working on a third. I'm painting more and more every day. I've still got dreams I know I will see come true and I'm not like everyone else, so why would I want to do it like everyone else? I wouldn't.

Those who really want to see me and be connected with me will find a way.

We are not the same.

I won't take my pages down because I have groups I admin but I won't be there very often. It doesn't give me pleasure and I've stopped doing things I hate.

I love you all so very much, we just can't be friends this way any longer.

All good things must come to an end and this thing stopped being good a long long time ago.

I will not live my life letting perfect strangers rip out my heart day after day. No one gets a say in who I am, what I believe or how I feel about life. It's my life to live, most are only in it through an internet connection.

They could block me out permanently any day, so good bye it was nice knowing you.

In Closing

I'm completely convinced I was off my rocker. It was difficult to go back through all of it. It's been a while since I wrote it and actually thought it go dumped.

I didn't feel the need to provide evidence or make any real argument against all of it. It is what it is.

It's not my life anymore, but I've shown it all to you and being a writer it's all there embarrassingly in black and white, the things I thought I believed.

I'm not that person any longer, I don't have the same situations, thoughts and or beliefs.

I'm finished talking about it now. There's nothing to go back to and everything in front of me. The hurt and anger have subsided and I cherish my few precious friends more than all those people put together.

I'm watching a great deconstruction go on with those who didn't get blocked along the way. They are still clinging to the hope there is a god, they still can't see their lives without him and or giving credit to that thought process.

I like my life. I spend a great deal of time talking to my plants, digging in the dirt and dreaming of a farming future.

I'm chasing those things, I'm not depending on anyone or a god to help me with it. I go out every day and try getting it one way or another.

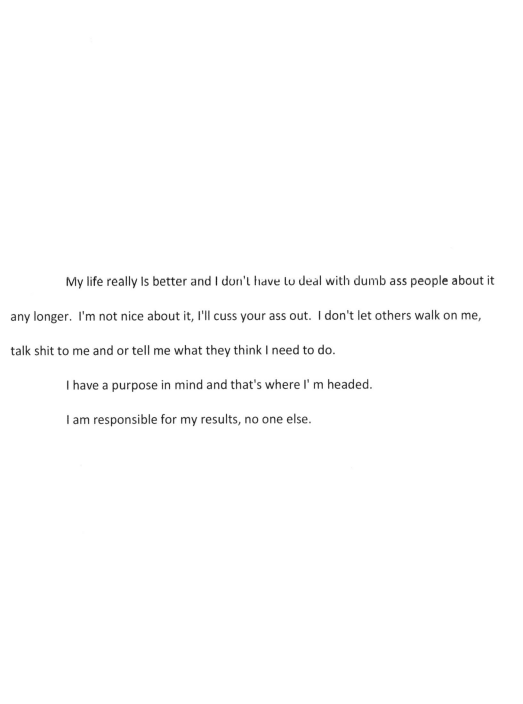

My life really Is better and I don't have to deal with dumb ass people about it any longer. I'm not nice about it, I'll cuss your ass out. I don't let others walk on me, talk shit to me and or tell me what they think I need to do.

I have a purpose in mind and that's where I' m headed.

I am responsible for my results, no one else.

Made in the USA
Middletown, DE
18 May 2023

30800617R00159